TOO GOOD TO WA$TE

THE AUSTRALIAN
Women's Weekly
HOW TO MAKE THE MOST OF YOUR GROCERIES
TOO GOOD TO WA$TE
RECIPES TO SAVE MONEY & SAVE THE PLANET
THE AUSTRALIAN WOMEN'S WEEKLY TEST KITCHEN
TEST KITCHEN TESTED

CONTENTS

FIGHT FOOD WASTE

If you have this cookbook, no doubt you're already looking for ways to reduce your impact on the planet. Perhaps you're also motivated to save money and experiment with new recipes. You might want to use less but get more out of your food. Maybe you're ready to transform your kitchen to zero-waste and say goodbye to excess packaging. Whatever your motivation is, this cookbook will help you get to where you want to be.

Have a think about why you chose this book. What is your personal motivation? What would you like to change about your relationship with the food you buy to eat?

If you can answer these questions, it will be easier to start your journey towards a new way of doing things. Like any change, it all starts with you, in your heart – and a willingness to believe that you can do things differently.

It will be worth it. Because food is too good to waste!

WHY SUSTAINABLE CHOICES MATTER

When it comes to food, the scale of waste across the globe is staggering. According to the Food and Agriculture Organization of the United Nations, approximately 45% of the world's fruit and vegetables are wasted each year. About one-third of the total amount of food produced goes to waste. Food waste also contributes to climate change and is responsible for approximately 8% of global greenhouse gas emissions. There's enough food to feed every person on the planet, but world hunger still affects millions of people. None of it really makes sense.

From the local to the global scale, there's obviously an urgent need to change how we do things. And every choice you make about food matters.

You can start by making a difference in your own home and kitchen. There are lots of ways to make more sustainable choices. You can choose to shop better and buy fair and ethical products. You can learn new ways to store your food and become skilled at clever ways of cooking. Better yet, you could even grow some of your own food or get to know your local farmers and farmers' markets.

While your actions might seem small or insignificant at first, when we all make better choices, they add up to create a better food system overall.

WHAT IS FOOD WASTE?

Food waste happens when we buy more than we need. It also happens when we don't store it correctly or don't eat it before it goes off. From bread, to vegetables, to leftovers, so much food ends up in the bin. We've all been there!

But it's not just about the food in your fridge. Food waste occurs along the whole production line. From the growing methods, to transporting, refrigerating and storing food, all the different stages have the potential to create waste.

The time, effort and resources that go into growing, storing and transporting food commercially across the globe is enormous. The way we grow and use our food has a huge impact on the health of people and the planet – and your hip pocket. Don't waste it!

WHY ZERO-WASTE & SUSTAINABLE IS THE WAY TO GO

We can all take action to reduce food waste and save money in our own homes.

Small changes can make a big difference, especially when they are all added up. Whether it's planning your meals, eating leftovers, being conscious of where your food comes from (and how it's packaged), or growing your own, all of these small changes make a difference. And the bonus is that you'll save money too.

Food waste is just a mindset. In the pages of this cookbook, you'll start to see food for what it is – a vital part of nature that can nourish your body and mind. In a circular food system, nothing goes to waste. You can learn how to put food scraps back into the earth through composting. It all starts with understanding that we are a part of nature, not the master of it. And we can learn much from First Nations peoples who knew how to respect and live within nature.

You can support ways of farming that improve the land like regenerative agriculture, food forests, biodynamics and permaculture. Healthy food comes from healthy soil, which has had minimal human intervention and has high nutritional value. When you buy healthy food that's been grown in a way that supports nature, you're also supporting a system that rebuilds our soil and increases our food security in a changing climate. By making mindful changes, you can help regenerate the earth, and inspire others too.

12 WAYS TO GET STARTED

It's time to reduce waste and rediscover the joy of connecting with your food. Here are 12 ways to get started. You'll learn more about each of these in the pages of this book.

Get to know your farmers and where your food was grown and how

Buy seasonally

Get into the garden and find the joy in growing your own

Store food properly to keep it fresh for longer

Only buy what you know you will eat

Start a compost or worm farm

Reduce packaging and processed foods

Plan your meals

Learn more about the food system so you can make informed choices

Ask businesses to stock food that is better for you and the planet

Share and swap food with neighbours

Join a farm-to-plate delivery service

USE IT ALL
USE IT ALL
USE IT ALL
USE IT ALL
USE IT ALL
USE IT ALL

PREP + COOK TIME 1 HOUR 40 MINUTES **SERVES** 8

BANANA DATE LOAF

TO MAKE THE BANANA LOAF VEGAN, USE MAPLE SYRUP OR RICE MALT SYRUP INSTEAD OF HONEY, AND A PLANT-BASED MILK MIXED WITH 1 TABLESPOON LEMON JUICE INSTEAD OF BUTTERMILK.

½ cup (55g) coarsely chopped mixed nuts
½ cup (45g) rolled oats
1 tbsp neutral oil, plus ⅓ cup (80ml) extra (see swap ins)
1 tbsp honey
1 tsp ground cinnamon
2 tbsp demerara sugar
3 small overripe bananas (390g), mashed, skins reserved (see waste not)
2 tsp vanilla extract
1¼ cups (310ml) buttermilk (see swap ins)
200g medjool dates, pitted, chopped coarsely (see swap ins)
2 cups (300g) self-raising flour
1 tsp bicarbonate of soda
1½ tsp baking powder
labne and honey, to serve (optional)

1 Preheat oven to 180°C/160°C fan-forced. Grease and line a 10cm x 20cm loaf pan.

2 Combine nuts, oats, oil and honey in a bowl. Place half the nut mixture on a lined oven tray. Bake for 10 minutes or until golden. Set aside to cool.

3 Meanwhile, combine cinnamon and sugar in a bowl.

4 Blend or process banana, vanilla, buttermilk and half the dates until smooth.

5 Sift flour, bicarb and baking powder into a large bowl, then add banana mixture, remaining dates, extra oil and roasted nut mixture; fold until just combined. Spoon banana mixture into the loaf pan and smooth the surface; sprinkle over remaining nut mixture and the cinnamon sugar.

6 Bake loaf for 1 hour 10 minutes or until a skewer inserted in the centre comes out clean. Cool in the pan for 15 minutes, then transfer to a wire rack to cool completely.

7 Serve loaf sliced, topped with labne and honey.

SWAP INS *Neutral oils include vegetable, sunflower, grapeseed, peanut and rice bran. Instead of buttermilk, you could use Greek yoghurt or combine 1¼ cups (310ml) milk with 1 tablespoon lemon juice. Swap the dates with other dried fruit, such as dried apricots or sultanas.*

WASTE NOT

RESERVE BANANA SKINS TO MAKE THE TURMERIC EGGPLANT CURRY, PAGE 13. STORE, COVERED, IN THE FRIDGE FOR UP TO 3 DAYS.

WASTE NOT

RESERVE ANY REMAINING LEMON SKINS TO MAKE THE CITRUS TEA JAM, PAGE 41. STORE, COVERED, IN THE FRIDGE FOR UP TO 4 DAYS.

PREP + COOK TIME 50 MINUTES **SERVES** 4

TURMERIC EGGPLANT CURRY

USE THIS VERSATILE CURRY PASTE WITH ANY MIX OF PROTEINS AND VEGETABLES TO CREATE YOUR OWN TAKE ON THIS VIBRANT AND FLAVOUR-PACKED DISH.

3 leftover banana skins (200g), cut into 2cm pieces
½ tsp bicarbonate of soda
¼ cup (60ml) coconut oil or ghee (see swap ins)
2 curry leaf sprigs, plus extra fried sprigs to serve (optional)
2 tsp brown mustard seeds
1 tsp cumin seeds
1 large eggplant (500g), cut into 3cm pieces
½ small cauliflower (500g), cut into small florets
2 long chillies, sliced thinly
400ml can coconut cream
2 tsp lemon juice (see waste not)
1 tsp caster sugar

CURRY PASTE

4 shallots (100g), chopped
2 tbsp finely grated fresh turmeric (see swap ins)
1 tbsp finely grated ginger
4 cloves garlic
1 tsp caster sugar
1 tsp salt
1 bunch coriander, stems and roots chopped, leaves reserved

1 Place banana skins in a medium bowl; sprinkle over bicarb and rub into skins. Cover with boiling water; stand for 15 minutes. Drain and rinse.

2 Meanwhile, make the curry paste: Blend or process ingredients until combined and smooth. Season with pepper. (Makes 180g.)

3 Heat coconut oil or ghee in a large saucepan over medium-high heat. Cook curry leaves, and mustard and cumin seeds for 1 minute or until crisp and fragrant. Using a slotted spoon, transfer to a plate.

4 Add eggplant to pan; cook, stirring occasionally, for 2 minutes or until golden. Add cauliflower, banana skins, the curry paste and half the chilli; cook, stirring, for 5 minutes or until the paste is fragrant and golden.

5 Add mustard and cumin seeds, crisp curry leaves, coconut cream and 1⅔ cups (410ml) water. Bring to the boil, then reduce heat to medium; simmer for 10 minutes or until vegetables are tender. Stir in lemon juice and sugar. Season to taste.

6 Top curry with remaining chilli and extra fried curry sprigs.

SWAP INS *Instead of coconut oil or ghee, you could use a neutral oil, such as vegetable, sunflower, peanut or rice bran oil. Instead of fresh turmeric, you could use 2 teaspoons ground turmeric.*

SERVING SUGGESTIONS
Serve curry topped with toasted shredded coconut, roasted cashews and chopped coriander, and with steamed jasmine rice and mini pappadums. You could also serve with mint, roasted peanuts or almonds and naan.

PREP + COOK TIME 2 HOURS 20 MINUTES (+ STANDING) **SERVES** 4

BUTTER BEAN STUFFED PUMPKIN

WHEN STORED IN A COOL, DARK AND DRY PLACE, A WHOLE PUMPKIN CAN LAST UP TO 6 MONTHS. BE SURE TO STAND IT ON A MAT OR PIECE OF CARDBOARD RATHER THAN DIRECTLY ON THE FLOOR.

---

4 slices bread (180g), torn coarsely (see swap ins)
2 tbsp olive oil
3.4kg whole Kent pumpkin
50g butter
1 medium onion (150g), sliced thinly
3 cloves garlic, crushed
2 tsp ground cumin
1 tsp chilli flakes
400g can butter beans, drained, rinsed (see swap ins)
¼ cup (40g) currants
200g fetta, crumbled
½ cup (80g) roasted almonds, chopped coarsely (see swap ins)
rocket leaves, to serve

CAPSICUM SAUCE

285g jar chargrilled capsicums, drained, patted dry
¾ cup (180g) sour cream (see swap ins)

1 Preheat oven to 180°C/160°C fan-forced.

2 Place bread on an oven tray lined with baking paper; drizzle over oil and season. Bake for 20 minutes or until golden and crisp.

3 Meanwhile, using a sharp knife, cut a 10cm round around the pumpkin stalk; using a spoon, lever the top off. Remove seeds and pulpy flesh from inside the pumpkin; reserve seeds (see waste not), and lid. Discard stringy pulp.

4 Melt butter in a frying pan over medium heat. Cook onion, stirring, for 8 minutes or until starting to soften. Stir in garlic, cumin and chilli flakes; cook for 2 minutes or until caramelised. Transfer to a large bowl.

5 Add toasted bread, beans, currants and half the fetta to the onion mixture; mix and scrunch with your hands until well combined. Season.

6 Fill the pumpkin cavity with the bread mixture, pressing down to firmly pack in. Place pumpkin on an oven tray lined with baking paper and cover with foil. Roast for 50 minutes. Add pumpkin lid to tray and roast for a further 40 minutes or until pumpkin is tender and centre of stuffing is hot. Stand for 10 minutes.

7 Meanwhile, make the capsicum sauce: Blend or process ingredients until smooth; season to taste. (Makes 1¾ cups.)

8 Cut pumpkin into wedges. Reserve 2 cups (580g) of the roast pumpkin flesh for a second meal, if desired (see waste not).

9 Top pumpkin wedges with remaining fetta, the almonds and rocket. Serve with stuffing and capsicum sauce.

SWAP INS *We've used sourdough, but use whichever bread you have on hand. Instead of butter beans, you could also use any variety of canned bean. Instead of almonds, use whichever nuts you have in your pantry. You could swap sour cream with Greek yoghurt, ricotta, cream cheese or cottage cheese.*

WASTE NOT

USE RESERVED PUMPKIN SEEDS AND PUMPKIN TO MAKE THE PUMPKIN SOUP WITH CANDIED SEEDS, PAGE 17. STORE, COVERED, IN THE FRIDGE FOR UP TO 3 DAYS.

SWAP INS

IF YOU DON'T HAVE RESERVED PUMPKIN SEEDS, YOU COULD USE STORE-BOUGHT PUMPKIN SEEDS, OR USE EXTRA NUTS. INSTEAD OF GREEK YOGHURT, YOU COULD USE ANY FORM OF CREAM OR A SOFT CHEESE SUCH AS RICOTTA.

PREP + COOK TIME 20 MINUTES **SERVES** 2

PUMPKIN SOUP WITH CANDIED SEEDS

A SIMPLE SOLUTION TO LEFTOVER ROASTED STARCHY VEGETABLES IS BLITZING THEM INTO A SOUP. PUMPKIN IS A CLASSIC FAVOURITE, BUT YOU COULD ALSO TRY SWEET POTATO OR CARROT.

2 tbsp olive oil
¼ cup (40g) mixed nuts
½ tsp nigella seeds
½ cup (45g) leftover pumpkin seeds (see swap ins)
1 tbsp honey
1 small onion (80g), chopped
2 cloves garlic, sliced
pinch ground cardamom
pinch ground cinnamon
2 cups (580g) leftover roast pumpkin (see tip)
½ cup (125ml) vegetable stock
¼ cup (70g) Greek yoghurt (see swap ins)
coriander or other soft leaf herb, to serve

1 Heat half the oil in a large frying pan over medium-high heat. Toast mixed nuts, nigella seeds and pumpkin seeds for 3 minutes or until golden. Stir in honey; cook for 1 minute or until caramelised. Transfer to a plate.

2 Heat the remaining oil in a medium saucepan over medium heat. Cook onion and garlic, stirring, for 5 minutes or until softened. Stir in cardamon and cinnamon, then add pumpkin, stock and 1 cup (250ml) water. Bring to the boil, then remove from heat.

3 Blend or process pumpkin mixture until smooth, adding extra water if too thick. Return soup to pan over medium heat; stir until hot. Season to taste.

4 Serve soup drizzled with yoghurt; top with candied seeds and coriander. Season with freshly ground pepper.

TIP *If you don't have leftover roast pumpkin, preheat oven to 200°C/180°C fan-forced. Place 500g coarsely chopped pumpkin on a lined oven tray; drizzle with 1 tablespoon olive oil and season. Roast for 25 minutes or until tender.*

PREP + COOK TIME 35 MINUTES **SERVES** 2

WHOLE BAKED TAHINI SNAPPER

THIS LEBANESE DISH, ALSO KNOWN AS SAMKEH HARRA, CAN BE ENJOYED AS IS OR SERVED ALONGSIDE TOASTED PITTA BREAD OR A ZINGY COUSCOUS SALAD.

2 cloves garlic
½ cup (125ml) lemon juice
¼ cup (70g) tahini
1 tsp sweet paprika
½ tsp chilli powder
1 tsp fine salt, plus extra pinch
2 tbsp olive oil
1kg whole snapper, cleaned
1 lemon, sliced thinly, plus extra wedges to serve
1 shallot, sliced thinly
pinch caster sugar
1 cup coriander and mint leaves and stems (see swap ins)
⅓ cup (50g) pine nuts, toasted (see swap ins)

1 Preheat oven to 200°C/180°C fan-forced.

2 Blend or process garlic, half the lemon juice, the tahini, paprika, chilli powder, salt and oil until smooth; season to taste.

3 Place fish on a foil-lined oven tray and rub with tahini mixture. Arrange lemon slices around and inside fish.

4 Bake fish for 20 minutes or until flesh flakes easily away from the bone. Reserve 200g cooked fish plus the head and bones for a second meal, if desired (see waste not).

5 Meanwhile, combine shallot, extra pinch of salt, the sugar and remaining lemon juice in a small bowl. Set aside to pickle. Drain before serving.

6 Top fish with pickled shallot, herbs and pine nuts. Serve with extra lemon wedges.

SWAP INS *Instead of coriander and mint, you could use parsley or dill. Swap pine nuts with almonds, walnuts or pistachios.*

WASTE NOT

USE THE RESERVED COOKED FISH AND BONES TO MAKE THE HARISSA FISH & TOMATO RISOTTO, PAGE 21. STORE, COVERED, IN THE FRIDGE FOR UP TO 1 DAY.

SWAP INS

INSTEAD OF CHERRY TOMATOES, YOU COULD ROAST ANY IN-SEASON VEGETABLE OF CHOICE. INSTEAD OF DILL, YOU CAN GARNISH WITH PARSLEY, CHIVES OR BASIL LEAVES.

PREP + COOK TIME 1 HOUR 25 MINUTES **SERVES** 4

HARISSA FISH & TOMATO RISOTTO

IF YOU DON'T HAVE FISH BONES TO MAKE THE STOCK, MAKE THE RISOTTO WITH 1 LITRE STORE-BOUGHT FISH STOCK. IF YOU HAVE ANY VEGETABLE PEELS, ADD TO THE STOCK FOR AN EXTRA FLAVOUR BOOST.

500g leftover fish head and bones
¼ cup (60ml) olive oil, plus extra to drizzle
1 lemon, sliced thinly
¼ tsp black peppercorns
250g cherry tomatoes (see swap ins)
1 tsp fine salt
1 shallot (25g), chopped finely
2 tbsp harissa paste
1½ cups (300g) arborio rice
200g leftover cooked fish (see tip)
dill fronds (see swap ins), finely grated lemon rind and lemon wedges, to serve

1 Preheat oven to 220°C/200°C fan-forced.

2 Place fish head and bones in a large casserole pot or ovenproof saucepan; drizzle with 1 tablespoon of the oil and season to taste. Roast for 20 minutes or until golden brown. Transfer the pot to the stove.

3 Immediately add 1.5 litres (6 cups) water, lemon slices and peppercorns. Heat stock mixture over medium heat. Bring to a simmer and cook for 20 minutes. Strain then return stock to pot or saucepan; season to taste. Discard fish head and bones. Keep stock warm over low heat.

4 Meanwhile, place tomatoes, the salt and 1 tablespoon of the oil in a medium baking dish. Roast for 15 minutes until tender and slightly charred.

5 Heat remaining oil in a large saucepan over medium heat. Cook shallot, stirring, for 4 minutes or until tender. Add harissa and cook, stirring, for 2 minutes until fragrant. Stir in rice and cook for 1 minute.

6 Add stock to rice, one ladle at a time, stirring after each addition. Add more stock when the majority has been absorbed. Continue for 25 minutes or until rice is al dente. Add fish and gently stir to combine; season.

7 Top risotto with roast tomatoes, dill fronds and lemon rind; season with freshly ground pepper and drizzle with extra olive oil. Serve with lemon wedges.

TIP *If you don't have leftover cooked fish, preheat oven to 200°C/180°C fan-forced. Bake 250g seasoned fish fillet of choice for 12 minutes or until just cooked through, then coarsely flake.*

PURCHASING POWER

Buying locally means purchasing in-season produce from growers and farmers within your local area. It's a small act but an act that reduces waste and positively reduces your environmental footprint. Depending on where you live, you can find local food at independent grocers and stores, farmers' markets, roadside stalls and even online businesses that deliver straight to your door.

In comparison, food bought out of season is likely to have been transported from miles away (or even overseas). This means higher food miles, more emissions, and a significant amount of food that is spoilt and wasted in the process.

It's a joy to get to know and support your local growers and farmers. Ask questions about where and how the produce was grown to make better purchasing decisions. This helps to strengthen food security, boost local economies and support our small-scale farmers. It also encourages backyard farmers to grow more food, making communities more resilient and self-sufficient. As a result, your food will be fresher and more nutritional.

Our fast-paced, industrial culture has escalated the convenience of fast and instantaneous food rather than healthy, ethical and slow wholefoods. Aim to purchase food that has been grown regeneratively. This practice of farming gives back to our earth and nourishes the soil, rather than taking from and depleting it like conventional methods of farming. By helping to store more carbon in the soil, this method of farming also helps to reverse climate change.

Our purchasing choices shape the world we see and the type of food that's available. Take it step-by-step and try some of these changes:

- Connect with your local farmers
- Ask stores to stock environment-friendly products
- Take your own reusable containers, bags and baskets to shops and farmers' markets
- Join with friends or neighbours to buy, grow, swap or share
- Buy in bulk to cut down on packaging
- Start growing some of your produce

PREP + COOK TIME 1 HOUR 55 MINUTES **SERVES** 4

CLASSIC ROAST CHICKEN & STUFFING

ADJUST STUFFING TO USE WHATEVER YOU HAVE AVAILABLE, SUCH AS SWAPPING HERBS AND NUTS OR USING PANCETTA, PROSCIUTTO OR CHORIZO IN PLACE OF BACON.

1.7kg whole chicken
60g butter, softened
2 tsp fine salt
2 tsp freshly ground black pepper
fried sage leaves, to serve (optional)

STUFFING

2 tbsp olive oil
125g butter, chopped
2 rashers bacon (80g), chopped
1 large onion (200g), chopped
300g mushrooms of choice, cut into small pieces
3 cloves garlic, crushed
2 tbsp sage leaves
2 tbsp thyme leaves
1 cup (70g) stale coarse breadcrumbs
1 cup (150g) cooked rice
½ cup parsley, chopped
¼ cup (40g) toasted pine nuts
1 lemon, rind grated finely, then juiced

1 Preheat oven to 200°C/180°C fan-forced.

2 Make the stuffing: Heat oil and butter in a large frying pan over medium heat. Cook bacon and onion, stirring, for 8 minutes or until onion is softened. Add mushrooms, garlic and herbs; cook, stirring, for 8 minutes or until tender. Add breadcrumbs, rice, parsley, pine nuts, and lemon rind and juice; stir until well combined. Season to taste.

3 Pat chicken dry inside and out with paper towel; place in a medium roasting tray. Fill cavity with stuffing. Tie legs together with kitchen string to enclose the stuffing. Reserve any remaining stuffing. Rub butter over skin and season with the salt and pepper.

4 Pour 1 cup (250ml) water into the roasting tray. Roast chicken, brushing occasionally with pan juices, for 50 minutes. Add remaining stuffing to tray. Return chicken to oven. Roast for 20 minutes or until chicken and stuffing are browned and juices run clear when the thickest part of a thigh is pierced. Cover with foil; rest for 15 minutes. Reserve 200g cooked chicken for a second meal, if desired (see waste not).

5 Serve chicken with stuffing and resting juices. Top with fried sage leaves.

SERVING SUGGESTION

Serve with Crisp-crushed Herby Potatoes, page 62, and a green leafy salad.

WASTE NOT

USE RESERVED ROAST CHICKEN TO MAKE THE TORTILLA CHICKEN SALAD, PAGE 27. STORE, COVERED, IN THE FRIDGE FOR UP TO 3 DAYS.

WASTE NOT

USE ANY REMAINING CABBAGE TO MAKE THE CHARRED CABBAGE WITH BLUE CHEESE DRESSING, PAGE 32, OR TOMATO & CABBAGE TABBOULEH, PAGE 35.

PREP + COOK TIME 30 MINUTES **SERVES** 2

TORTILLA CHICKEN SALAD

THIS CRUNCHY SALAD IS A PERFECT LIGHT MEAL. IF YOU'RE MISSING SOME OF THE FRESH VEGETABLES, REPLACE WITH WHICHEVER FRESH SALAD INGREDIENTS YOU HAVE ON HAND.

1 clove garlic, crushed
1 long chilli, chopped finely, plus extra sliced to serve
1 lime, rind grated finely, then juiced, plus extra wedges to serve
⅓ cup (80ml) olive oil
1 small red onion (80g), sliced thinly
1 tsp ground cumin
2 x 15cm stale corn tortillas, (see swap ins)
1 bulb baby fennel (130g), fronds reserved
1 small bunch radishes (230g), leaves attached and reserved
¼ small red cabbage (300g), sliced thinly (see waste not)
1 medium avocado (250g), sliced
200g leftover roast chicken, shredded coarsely (see tip)
1 cup coriander stems and leaves, chopped coarsely, plus extra leaves to serve

1 Combine garlic, chilli, lime rind and juice, and half the oil in a small bowl; season to taste. Add onion and set aside.

2 Combine cumin and remaining oil in another small bowl; season to taste.

3 Brush cumin oil over both sides of tortillas. Heat a large frying pan over high heat. Cook each tortilla, turning, for 2 minutes, or until golden and crisp. Drain on paper towel.

4 Using a mandoline, V-slicer or sharp knife, thinly slice fennel and radishes; place in a large bowl. Add reserved fennel fronds and radish leaves, the cabbage, avocado, chicken, coriander and lime dressing with onion; toss to combine. Season to taste.

5 Break crisp tortillas over salad and season with freshly ground pepper. Serve with extra lime wedges, sliced chilli and coriander leaves.

TIP *If you don't have any leftover roast chicken, heat 1 tablespoon oil in a frying pan. Cook 250g seasoned chicken breast or thigh fillet, turning, for 10–12 minutes or until cooked through. Cool for 5 minutes then shred. Alternatively, you can use another protein, such as prawns, sliced beef steak or firm tofu.*

SWAP INS *Instead of corn tortillas you could also use flatbreads, corn chips or bread toasted into croûtons.*

PREP + COOK TIME 1 HOUR 10 MINUTES **SERVES** 4

BRAISED CELERY WITH NUT PICADA

THE STURDY, SLIGHTLY MORE BITTER OUTER STALKS OF CELERY PROTECT ITS CENTRAL TENDER HEART. SLOW COOKING THESE OUTER STALKS BRINGS OUT THEIR NATURAL SWEETNESS.

1 head of celery (1.5kg)
2 cups (500ml) dry white wine
2 cups (500ml) olive oil
1 tbsp finely grated lemon rind (see waste not)
⅓ cup (80ml) lemon juice
6 sprigs thyme
3 cloves garlic, bruised
1 tbsp Dijon mustard
150g goat's curd
2 tbsp currants (see swap ins)

NUT PICADA

2 slices bread (90g), torn coarsely (see swap ins)
⅓ cup (50g) mixed nuts, chopped coarsely (see swap ins)
1 clove garlic, crushed
1 tbsp thyme leaves
2 tbsp olive oil
¼ cup parsley stems and leaves, chopped finely
1 tbsp finely grated lemon rind

1 Preheat oven to 160°C/140°C fan-forced.

2 Reserve 3 celery stalks (150g) and 1 cup celery leaves for a second meal, if desired (see waste not). Using a mandoline, V-slicer or sharp knife, thinly slice celery heart. Trim and slice remaining celery outer stalks into 10cm lengths. Reserve remaining leaves.

3 Place wine, oil, lemon rind and juice, thyme, garlic and 1 cup (250ml) water in a large saucepan; stir to combine. Season to taste. Bring to a simmer over medium-high heat. Add outer celery stalks. Reduce heat to low-medium. Cook for 50 minutes or until celery is tender. Set aside to cool. Reserve ¼ cup (60ml) braising liquid in a small bowl.

4 Meanwhile, make the nut picada: Place bread, nuts, garlic, thyme and oil on a lined oven tray; toss to combine. Season to taste. Bake for 15 minutes until golden brown. Cool. Add parsley and lemon rind; toss to combine.

5 Add mustard to reserved braising liquid and whisk to combine; season to taste.

6 To serve, spread goat's curd over a platter; top with braised and sliced celery, currants, nut picada and reserved celery leaves. Drizzle with mustard dressing.

SWAP INS *Instead of currants you could also use sultanas or raisins. We've used sourdough, but use whichever bread you have on hand. You can use any nuts you have for this recipe; we used hazelnuts, pistachios and walnuts.*

SERVING SUGGESTIONS
Serve as a starter or light meal, or with cooked grains or legumes.

WASTE NOT

USE THE RESERVED CELERY AND CELERY LEAVES TO MAKE THE SPEEDY SPICY CELERY RELISH, PAGE 31; STORE, COVERED, IN THE FRIDGE FOR UP TO 1 WEEK. KEEP ANY REMAINING LEMON SKINS TO MAKE THE CITRUS TEA JAM, PAGE 41; STORE, COVERED, IN THE FRIDGE FOR UP TO 4 DAYS.

WASTE NOT

RESERVE YOUR PEELED GINGER SKIN TO MAKE THE VEGETABLE STOCK, PAGE 54, OR DEHYDRATE TO MAKE A FLAVOURED SALT, PAGE 49.

PREP + COOK TIME 20 MINUTES (+ COOLING) **MAKES** 2 CUPS

SPEEDY SPICY CELERY RELISH

THERE ARE ENDLESS OPTIONS FOR THIS BRIGHT AND EARTHY RELISH – SPOON OVER RICE, NOODLES AND EGGS, OR SERVE ALONGSIDE PROTEINS SUCH AS STEAMED FISH, PORK OR SILKEN TOFU.

3 stalks (150g) leftover celery, sliced thinly
1 cup leftover celery leaves, chopped finely
2 green onions (20g), sliced thinly
2 long green chillies, sliced thinly
1 bunch coriander, stems and leaves chopped coarsely
50g fresh ginger, peeled, sliced thinly (see waste not)
3 cloves garlic, sliced thinly
¾ cup (185ml) neutral oil (see tip)
1 tbsp sesame oil
1½ tbsp rice wine vinegar (see swap ins)
1½ tsp fine salt
2 tsp Sichuan peppercorns, crushed (see swap ins)
½ tsp caster sugar

1 Place celery stalks and leaves, green onion, chilli and coriander in a large bowl; toss to combine.

2 Place ginger, garlic and neutral oil in a small saucepan over low heat; cook for 4 minutes or until garlic and ginger are golden. Remove from heat. Strain oil through a fine sieve into a jug; reserve garlic and ginger. Set aside for 10 minutes to cool slightly.

3 Pour infused oil over celery mixture. Add sesame oil, vinegar, the salt, peppercorns, sugar, and reserved garlic and ginger; stir to combine. Season to taste.

4 Transfer relish to a clean container or jar. Store in the fridge for up to 4 days.

TIP *Neutral oils include vegetable, sunflower, grapeseed, peanut and rice bran.*

SWAP INS *Instead of rice wine vinegar you could also use apple cider vinegar, Chinese black vinegar or white wine vinegar. You can replace Sichuan peppercorns with a combination of freshly ground black peppercorns and coriander seeds, if you like.*

PREP + COOK TIME 30 MINUTES **SERVES** 4 (AS A SIDE)

CHARRED CABBAGE WITH BLUE CHEESE DRESSING

CHOOSE FROM WHOLE STURDY RED OR GREEN CABBAGES, OR OPT FOR THE MORE DELICATE SAVOY VARIETY. IF YOU PREFER A MILDER CHEESE TO BLUE CHEESE, YOU COULD USE FETTA, GOAT'S CHEESE OR ANY OTHER SOFT CHEESE.

⅓ cup (80ml) olive oil
1 tbsp fennel seeds, crushed lightly
1 tsp fine salt
1 whole medium cabbage (1.5kg) (see note above)
⅓ cup (50g) toasted pine nuts (see swap ins)
1 cup loosely packed red-veined sorrel leaves (see swap ins)

DRESSING

75g soft blue cheese (see note above)
½ cup (125ml) buttermilk (see swap ins)

1 Make the dressing: Blend or process ingredients until smooth. Season to taste.

2 Combine oil, fennel seeds and salt in a small bowl.

3 Preheat a grill plate or barbecue. Reserve 4 cabbage outer leaves for a second meal, if desired (see waste not). Halve cabbage lengthways; cut each half into six wedges, making sure each wedge is held together by the core. Brush each cabbage wedge with fennel oil and season with black pepper.

4 Cook cabbage on grill plate or barbecue for 10 minutes each side or until grill marks appear and cabbage is just tender. Finely shred any leaves that separate from the wedges. Reserve 4 cabbage wedges for a second meal, if desired (see waste not).

5 Drizzle dressing over charred cabbage; top with shredded cabbage, pine nuts and sorrel.

SWAP INS *Instead of pine nuts, you could use any variety of nut or seed. Instead of sorrel, you could use spinach, rocket or mixed leaves. Instead of buttermilk, you could use Greek yoghurt or combine ½ cup (125ml) milk with 2 teaspoons of lemon juice.*

SERVING SUGGESTIONS
Serve with grilled proteins or cooked grains, such as freekeh, couscous or wild rice.

WASTE NOT

USE RESERVED CABBAGE LEAVES AND WEDGES TO MAKE THE TOMATO & CABBAGE TABBOULEH, PAGE 35. STORE, COVERED, IN THE FRIDGE FOR UP TO 3 DAYS.

PREP + COOK TIME 15 MINUTES (+ STANDING) **SERVES** 4

TOMATO & CABBAGE TABBOULEH

TO CELEBRATE SEASONAL PRODUCE, YOU MAY NEED TO SWAP TOMATOES FOR MORE ABUNDANT OR AVAILABLE PRODUCE, SUCH AS RADISHES, ASPARAGUS OR BROCCOLI.

½ cup (80g) burghul (see swap ins)
250g leftover grilled cabbage wedges (see tip)
1 shallot, sliced thinly
500g tomatoes, cut into wedges
1 cup mint leaves (see swap ins)
¼ cup dill fronds (see swap ins)
1 long green or red chilli, sliced thinly
2 tbsp vinegar (see swap ins)
¼ cup (60ml) olive oil, plus extra to drizzle
4 leftover cabbage outer leaves
hummus, sumac, chargrilled flatbreads and lemon wedges, to serve (optional)

1 Place burghul and ¾ cup (180ml) boiling water in a bowl; stir to combine. Cover and set aside for 20 minutes or until water is absorbed.

2 Slice cabbage wedges thinly and add to burghul with shallot, tomatoes, herbs, chilli, vinegar and oil; toss to combine. Season to taste.

3 Fill outer cabbage leaves with tabbouleh, then top with a spoonful of hummus, a drizzle of extra olive oil and a dusting of sumac. Place remaining hummus in a small serving bowl. Serve with flatbreads and lemon wedges.

TIP *If you don't have leftover grilled cabbage, coarsely chopped ¼ cabbage (160g) and cook with 1 tablespoon olive oil in a large frying over high heat for 6 minutes or until tender; season to taste.*

SWAP INS *Instead of burghul, you could use couscous, rice or any other nutty grain. Swap mint and dill with parsley, basil, chives or coriander. We used white wine vinegar, but use whichever vinegar you have on hand.*

NOSE TO TAIL, ROOT TO TIP

Our social conventions place a taboo on eating certain foods and different parts of plants or animals so that we don't eat them in their entirety. This has resulted in a substantial amount of nutritious and edible food going to waste, and difficulty in sourcing the whole plant or animal, as meals containing anything other than perfect-looking produce and prime cuts are less appealing to the buyer's eye.

Through modifying the environment and selective breeding, humans have cultivated and changed food; beautiful heirloom varieties of vegetables are often quite hard to source and are quite different from what you see on major supermarkets' shelves.

Most parts of many plants and animals can in fact be eaten – and they provide health benefits and nutrients not often found in other foods. With an open mind, by increasing the diversity of the food you eat, not only will you reduce waste but you'll save money too.

WASTE NOT

Do you throw away the oil in the bottom of your sardine tin? Chuck out the parmesan rind or the bones from the Sunday roast? Use oils to cook off onion and garlic for sauces, and use rinds and bones to boost soups and stews. Use every last little bit.

FORAGING FEAST

Many so-called 'weeds' are edible and contain a high level of nutrition and health benefits. Keep an eye out for citrus and nut trees too. Caution: Always be sure to check what's edible – don't eat plants from roadsides as they may be sprayed with chemicals.

SUPER STOCKS

Don't buy stock from the supermarket. Make your own nutritious beef, chicken, or vegetable stock using leftovers and scraps (see page 54). This is a great way to reduce food waste. Simply keep them in your freezer until you have enough to cook with.

EAT YOUR LEAVES

Try eating and cooking with leaves. Save the leaves from veg such as beetroot, sweet potato, carrots, leeks, broccoli, radish and squash, and use as you would with other leafy greens. Experiment with edible flowers like zucchini flowers and nasturtiums.

MAKE THE MOST OF MEATS

Talk to your local butcher and experiment with using different cuts of meat. Try out new recipes to make use of less desired cuts. Find out what health benefits the different animal parts have and eat to your body's requirements.

POWER OF PLANTS

Think outside the square when it comes to plants. There are many weeds, seeds, skins, rinds and roots that can be eaten. Sprouts are a great way to maximise food efficiency, as they are highly nutritious, cheap, easy to grow and fun for the kids.

PREP + COOK TIME 1 HOUR 40 MINUTES (+ REFRIGERATION & COOLING) **SERVES** 10–12

ORANGE & ALMOND THYME CAKE

YOU WILL NEED ABOUT 4 MEDIUM ORANGES (960G) IN TOTAL; RESERVE THE SKINS TO MAKE THE CITRUS TEA JAM, PAGE 41. YOU COULD ALSO USE OTHER CITRUS, SUCH AS LEMON, GRAPEFRUIT OR A COMBINATION.

275g butter, chopped
1 tbsp chopped thyme, plus extra leaves to serve
2 tbsp finely grated orange rind (see note above)
6 eggs
260g roasted almond meal (see swap ins)
100g self-raising flour
1½ cups (330g) caster sugar
½ tsp fine salt
labne and toasted flaked almonds, to serve

ORANGE CURD

2 eggs
4 egg yolks (see waste not)
½ cup (110g) caster sugar
2 tbsp finely grated orange rind (see note above)
½ cup (125ml) orange juice (see note above)
125g unsalted butter, chopped

ORANGE CARAMEL

¾ cup (165g) caster sugar
½ cup (125ml) orange juice (see note above)

1 Make the orange curd: Place whole eggs, yolks, sugar, and orange rind and juice in a medium saucepan; whisk until combined. Add butter and cook over medium heat, whisking continuously, for 5 minutes or until sugar dissolves and mixture thickens. Remove from heat; strain through a sieve into a bowl. Cover curd surface directly; refrigerate for 3 hours or overnight to thicken and set.

2 Preheat oven to 180°C/160°C fan-forced. Grease and line a 22cm round cake pan.

3 Melt butter with thyme and orange rind in a medium saucepan over low heat. Set aside for 10 minutes to cool slightly, then whisk in eggs.

4 Combine almond meal, flour, sugar and salt in a large bowl. Add thyme butter mixture and whisk until just combined. Pour batter into cake pan.

5 Bake cake for 50 minutes or until a skewer inserted into the centre comes out clean. Cool in pan for 20 minutes, then transfer to a wire rack to cool completely.

6 Meanwhile, make the orange caramel: Place sugar and 2 tablespoons water in medium saucepan. Cook over medium heat, stirring, until sugar dissolves. Bring to the boil; cook, without stirring, for 5 minutes or until a deep caramel colour. Remove from heat, allow bubbles to subside, then add orange juice and 2 tablespoons water. Return to medium-high heat. Bring to the boil; cook, stirring, until smooth. Set aside to cool.

7 Spread labne over cake, then drizzle with caramel; top with flaked almonds and extra thyme leaves. Serve with curd.

SWAP INS *Instead of the almond meal, you could use another ground nut flour, polenta or plain flour.*

WASTE NOT

KEEP LEFTOVER EGG WHITES TO MAKE THE CRISP-CRUSHED HERBY POTATOES, PAGE 62. STORE REMAINING CURD, COVERED, IN THE FRIDGE FOR UP TO 1 MONTH; SERVE WITH DESSERTS OR SWEET BREAKFASTS.

SWAP INS

* * *

INSTEAD OF EARL GREY TEA, YOU COULD USE ANY OTHER BLACK TEA, SUCH AS ENGLISH BREAKFAST, DARJEELING OR CHAI. INSTEAD OF VERJUICE, YOU COULD ALSO USE APPLE CIDER VINEGAR OR WHITE WINE VINEGAR.

PREP + COOK TIME 1 HOUR 45 MINUTES **MAKES** 3½ CUPS (980G)

CITRUS TEA JAM

SIMILAR TO BUT LESS FUSSY THAN A MARMALADE, THIS ZESTY TEA-SPIKED JAM USES LEFTOVER CITRUS SKINS, SUCH AS ORANGE, LEMON, LIME OR GRAPEFRUIT.

4 leftover orange skins, quartered (see note above)
4 earl grey tea bags (see swap ins)
2 cups (440g) caster sugar
1½ cups (375ml) verjuice (see swap ins)
½ cup (175g) honey

1 Place orange skins and 1 litre (4 cups) water in a medium saucepan; bring to the boil over high heat. Reduce heat to medium. Cook, covered, for 20 minutes or until skins are softened. Transfer 2 cups (500ml) cooking liquid to a medium bowl, then drain. Set skins aside to cool slightly.

2 Add tea bags to reserved cooking liquid; steep for 15 minutes. Discard tea bags.

3 Blend or process the orange skins and sugar until almost smooth; transfer to a large saucepan.

4 Add verjuice, honey and tea mixture to the orange mixture; bring to the boil over high heat. Reduce heat to low-medium. Cook, stirring occasionally, for 1 hour or until thickened to a jam-like consistency.

5 Transfer jam to sterilised jars (see page 160). Store in the fridge for up to 1 month.

SERVING SUGGESTIONS

Serve on toasted or fresh bread alongside a pot of the same flavoured tea used to infuse your jam.

INFUSED OILS & VINEGARS

USE ANY ODD HERBS, PEELS AND SPICES TO CREATE YOUR OWN INFUSED OILS AND VINEGARS. MIX ANY OF THE FLAVOURINGS FOR A MORE COMPLEX RESULT, THEN USE TO LIVEN UP MARINADES, DRESSINGS AND SAUCES.

INFUSED OIL

Here the oil is heated to create a quicker infusion, though flavourings can be added at room temperature and allowed to sit for longer. For the best results, use a good-quality olive oil as your base oil.

Add flavourings to a sterilised jar or bottle (see page 160). Place enough oil in a saucepan to cover the flavourings; heat over low heat until just warmed, then pour oil over flavourings. Secure lid and set aside in a dark place for 1 week. Taste, and when flavour is to your liking, strain the oil into another sterilised jar or bottle.

INFUSED VINEGAR

We've used white wine vinegar, which is a versatile neutral base, but you could also use red wine vinegar, apple cider vinegar, white vinegar or rice wine vinegar, if preferred.

Add flavourings to a sterilised jar or bottle (see page 160); pour over enough vinegar to cover the flavourings. Secure lid and set aside for 2 weeks. Taste, and when flavour is to your liking, strain the vinegar into another sterilised jar or bottle.

FLAVOURINGS

HERBS

Lightly bruise herbs to release their natural oils. Use room-temperature oil for soft herbs.

Woody herbs: rosemary, thyme, sage, oregano, marjoram and bay leaves.

Soft herbs: basil, chives, dill, mint, tarragon, coriander and parsley.

CITRUS & FRUIT

Use any of the skin, peel or flesh. Fruit and berries are best used in an infused vinegar.

Lemon, lime, oranges, mandarins, grapefruit, ginger, lemongrass, berries, stone fruit, apples, pears, melon, pomegranate and pineapple.

SPICES

Lightly toast spices in a dry frying pan until fragrant before adding to oil or vinegar.

Peppercorns, star anise, cumin seeds, fennel seeds, mustard seeds, sesame seeds, chilli flakes and whole fresh or dried chillies.

PREP + COOK TIME 1 HOUR **SERVES** 4

CRISPY VEGIE & HALOUMI PARMIGIANA

HERE WE KEEP THE CAULIFLOWER LEAVES INTACT FOR EXTRA COLOUR AND CRUNCH. YOU COULD ALSO SAVE THE CAULIFLOWER LEAVES AND USE AS YOU WOULD KALE OR SILVERBEET.

1.8kg (4lb) cauliflower, leaves intact, or broccoli, cut into large wedges
2½ cups (500g) puffed millet (see swap ins)
½ cup (50g) walnuts (see swap ins)
½ cup parsley, stems and leaves (see swap ins)
250g haloumi, grated coarsely
¾ cup (115g) plain flour
4 eggs, beaten lightly
½ cup (125ml) olive oil
400g jar pasta sauce
pesto (see page 96) or your favourite condiment, and basil leaves, to serve

1 Preheat oven to 180°C/160°C fan-forced.

2 Cook cauliflower or broccoli in a large saucepan of salted boiling water for 8 minutes or until just tender. Drain then cool under cold water; pat dry. Reserve 500g cauliflower or broccoli to make a second meal, if desired (see waste not).

3 Meanwhile, process millet, walnuts, parsley and half the haloumi until well combined and chopped; season. Place flour, egg and millet mixture in separate wide bowls. Toss cauliflower or broccoli in flour to coat; shake to remove excess. Dip into egg to coat, then press into millet mixture until well coated. Transfer to a plate. Repeat with remaining cauliflower or broccoli.

4 Heat oil in a large, deep frying pan over medium-high heat. Cook cauliflower or broccoli, in batches, for 2 minutes each side or until golden. Drain on paper towel.

5 Place cauliflower or broccoli in a medium baking dish; spoon over pasta sauce and top with remaining haloumi. Bake for 20 minutes or until golden brown.

6 Serve parmigiana topped with spoonfuls of pesto and basil leaves.

TIP *Refrigerate any leftover pesto, covered in a thin layer of oil, for up to 2 days, or freeze for up to 2 months.*

SWAP INS *Instead of puffed millet, you could use puffed quinoa, puffed rice or mixed seeds. Instead of walnuts, you could use almonds, pine nuts or cashews. Swap parsley with whichever soft herbs you have on hand.*

WASTE NOT

✱ ✱ ✱

USE THE RESERVED CAULIFLOWER OR BROCCOLI TO MAKE THE VEGIE SEED-KOFTA PLATTER, PAGE 47. STORE, COVERED, IN THE FRIDGE FOR UP TO 3 DAYS.

SWAP INS

✸ ✸ ✸

WE USED RED WINE VINEGAR, BUT USE WHICHEVER VINEGAR YOU HAVE ON HAND. INSTEAD OF PSYLLIUM HUSKS, YOU COULD USE LINSEEDS, CHIA SEEDS OR ALMOND MEAL.

PREP + COOK TIME 1 HOUR 15 MINUTES **SERVES** 6 (MAKES 30 KOFTA)

VEGIE SEED-KOFTA PLATTER

ALONG WITH LEFTOVER CAULIFLOWER OR BROCCOLI, THIS RECIPE IS ALSO A GREAT OPPORTUNITY TO USE UP ANY ODD NUTS AND SEEDS TO BULK OUT AND FLAVOUR THE FRITTERS.

1 small red onion (100g), sliced thinly
¼ cup (60ml) vinegar (see swap ins)
250g seed mix (see tips), plus extra to serve
1½ tbsp cumin seeds
1½ tbsp coriander seeds
500g leftover cooked cauliflower or broccoli
½ cup mint, stems and leaves, loosely packed
2 cloves garlic
1 tbsp lemon juice
½ cup (140g) tahini
2 tbsp psyllium husks (see swap ins)
neutral oil, for deep-frying (see tips)
200g fetta, crumbled
½ cup parsley, stems and leaves
lemon wedges, to serve

BEETROOT HUMMUS
400g can chickpeas, drained, rinsed
4 vacuum-packed cooked baby beetroot (250g)
1 tbsp tahini
1 clove garlic
1 tbsp lemon juice
⅓ cup (80ml) olive oil

1 Make the beetroot hummus: Reserve ¼ cup of the chickpeas. Blend or process remaining chickpeas, the beetroot, tahini, garlic and lemon juice until well combined. With the motor running, gradually add oil and process until smooth; season to taste.

2 Place onion and vinegar in a small bowl. Set aside for 30 minutes to pickle. Drain.

3 Meanwhile, heat a medium frying pan over medium-high heat. Toast seed mix with cumin and coriander seeds, stirring, for 2 minutes or until seeds are golden.

4 Blend or process toasted seeds, cauliflower or broccoli, ¼ cup (60ml) water, mint, garlic, lemon juice, tahini and psyllium husks until a coarse paste forms; season.

5 Shape heaped tablespoons of the kofta mixture into ovals and place on a tray lined with baking paper.

6 Fill a medium saucepan two-thirds full with oil; heat to 160°C (or until the oil sizzles when a small cube of bread is added). Working in batches, fry kofta, turning occasionally, for 5 minutes or until dark golden and cooked through. Remove with a slotted spoon; drain on paper towel.

7 Serve kofta and hummus on a platter, topped with reserved chickpeas, extra seed mix, the fetta, pickled red onion and parsley. Serve with lemon wedges.

TIPS *We used a combination of pepitas, sunflower seeds, sesame seeds and linseeds. Instead of seeds, you could use whichever nuts you have on hand. Use any neutral oil of your choice, such as vegetable, sunflower, grapeseed, peanut and rice bran.*

GINGER & CURRY POWDER
TOMATO & BASIL
BEETROOT & ONION

FLAVOURED SALTS

USE THIS EASY TECHNIQUE TO PRESERVE EXCESS PRODUCE THAT CAN THEN BE USED TO CREATE FLAVOURED SALTS – PERFECT TO ENHANCE SAUCES, MEATS, SALADS AND MORE.

1 Preheat dehydrator or oven to 60°C/40°C fan-forced. Slice produce (see tip) very thinly using a mandoline, V-slicer or small, sharp knife; arrange on dehydrator racks or wire oven racks. Dehydrate in dehydrator or oven, with the door propped open, for 6–12 hours or until completely dried through.

2 Blend or process dried ingredients to a coarse powder; rub in 1 cup (125g) sea salt flakes. Store in a clean airtight jar for up to 3 months.

TIP *For our flavoured salts, we made: ginger & curry powder using 60g peeled, sliced ginger and 2 teaspoons curry powder; tomato & basil using 1 large thinly sliced tomato and 1 cup basil leaves; and beetroot & onion using ½ medium thinly sliced beetroot and 2 thinly sliced eschalots.*

SALT COMBINATIONS

ginger & curry powder
tomato & basil
beetroot & onion
lime & paprika
ginger & lime
mint & lime rind
lemon & black pepper
mushroom & rosemary
garlic & celery
dill, fennel & orange

PREP + COOK TIME 1 HOUR 30 MINUTES **SERVES** 4

GRILLED PINEAPPLE WITH RUM SYRUP

YOU COULD SPRINKLE FLAVOURED SALTS (PAGE 49) OVER THE PINEAPPLE, SUCH AS MINT & LIME RIND.

2 small pineapples (1.8kg)
6 whole star anise
⅔ cup (150g) caster sugar
1 cup (250ml) rum (see swap ins)
100g butter, chopped
mint leaves, lime wedges and ice-cream, to serve

1 Preheat a grill plate or barbecue. Preheat oven to 200°C/180°C fan-forced.

2 Peel and trim pineapples; reserve the peel and trimmings for another recipe, if desired (see waste not). Halve pineapples lengthways; cut each half into four wedges. Cut the core from each piece and reserve for the syrup.

3 Crush star anise using a mortar and pestle (see tip). Place ¼ cup (60ml) water, star anise, sugar and reserved pineapple cores in a medium saucepan; cook, stirring, over low heat until sugar is dissolved. Increase heat to medium. Cook, without stirring, swirling pan occasionally, for 15 minutes or until caramel is golden brown.

4 Meanwhile, cook pineapple wedges on a heated grill plate or barbecue for 1 minute each side or until grill marks appear. Transfer to a tray lined with baking paper.

5 Carefully add ¾ cup (180ml) of the rum to the hot caramel. Increase heat to high; boil for 2 minutes or until syrupy. Add butter and 1 cup (250ml) water; boil for 10 minutes or until thickened. Add remaining rum; cook for 2 minutes. Strain into a heatproof bowl; discard solids.

6 Brush grilled pineapple with rum syrup. Roast, basting every 10 minutes with the syrup, for 45 minutes or until tender and caramelised. Set aside to cool slightly.

7 Spoon roasting juices over pineapple. Serve with mint leaves, lime wedges, ice-cream and any remaining syrup.

TIP *If you don't have a mortar and pestle, use the base of a saucepan to crush the star anise.*

SWAP INS *Instead of rum, you could use brandy, bourbon or cognac.*

WASTE NOT

USE THE RESERVED PINEAPPLE PEEL TO MAKE THE DRINK PINEAPPLE TEPACHE, PAGE 53. STORE, COVERED, IN THE FRIDGE FOR UP TO 3 DAYS.

PREP + COOK TIME 20 MINUTES (+ 2–6 DAYS FERMENTING) **MAKES** 3 LITRES (12 CUPS)

PINEAPPLE TEPACHE

THIS MEXICAN FERMENTED DRINK IS MADE WITH JUST PINEAPPLE OFFCUTS AND BROWN SUGAR. MAKE THE BASE AND THEN FLAVOUR ACCORDING TO WHAT YOU HAVE AVAILABLE.

1 cup (220g) brown sugar
3 cups (800g) leftover pineapple peel and trimmings, washed well, chopped coarsely
pineapple wedges, to serve (optional)

FLAVOURINGS (OPTIONAL)
3 large ginger skin peels
2 tsp crushed juniper berries
1 cinnamon stick
1 small red chilli, halved lengthways

1 Bring 2 litres (8 cups) water to the boil in a medium saucepan; remove from heat. Stir in sugar until dissolved. Set aside to cool completely.

2 Place leftover pineapple peel and trimmings in a sterilised 3-litre jar (see page 160). If using flavourings, add ginger peel and juniper berries to the jar.

3 Place a small ramekin or pickle weight in the jar to weigh down the pineapple. Pour over the sugar-water mixture, ensuring the pineapple is completely submerged.

4 Cover jar with a clean tea towel or chux cloth; seal with a rubber band. Stand in a dark place for 1–3 days to ferment or until the surface has bubbles and there is a yeast-like aroma.

5 Strain tepache through a fine sieve into a clean jar; discard solids. If using flavourings, add cinnamon and chilli. Cover with a clean tea towel or chux cloth; seal with a rubber band. Stand in a dark place for another 1–3 days or until fizzy.

6 Serve tepache chilled: pour over ice in serving glasses with a wedge of pineapple, or store in the fridge for up to 2 weeks.

SERVING SUGGESTIONS
You could use tepache as a cocktail or mocktail mixer. If you prefer it less sweet, dilute with soda water.

STOCKS

KEEP VEGETABLE SCRAPS AND MEAT BONES OR OFFCUTS TO MAKE THESE NOURISHING BASES. VEGETABLE SCRAPS COULD INCLUDE CARROT PEELS, LEEK, GREEN ONION, CELERY OR FENNEL ENDS, KALE OR MUSHROOM STALKS AND ONION OR GARLIC SKINS. IF YOU'RE SHORT ON STORAGE SPACE, REDUCE THE STOCKS TO CONCENTRATES AND DILUTE WITH EXTRA WATER WHEN COOKING. USE THESE QUANTITIES AS A GUIDE TO SHAPE YOUR HOMEMADE STOCK.

FISH STOCK

PREP + COOK TIME
1 HOUR 10 MINUTES
MAKES 8 CUPS

Heat 2 tablespoons olive oil in a large saucepan over medium heat. Cook 1kg white fish bones, 2 cups (300g) mixed vegetable scraps and 1 tablespoon tomato paste (optional) for 5 minutes or until fragrant. Add 1 cup (250ml) dry white wine, 2.5 litres (10 cups) water, ½ teaspoon black peppercorns and 1 bunch (30g) parsley, tarragon or dill stalks. Bring to a gentle simmer over low heat; cook for 1 hour or until fragrant. Cool completely; strain using a fine sieve. Store in the fridge for up to 5 days or freeze for up to 3 months.

TIP *Use the fishbones from the Whole Baked Tahini Snapper on page 18, or ask your fishmonger for bones.*

CHICKEN STOCK

PREP + COOK TIME
1 HOUR 45 MINUTES
MAKES 8 CUPS

Heat 2 tablespoons olive oil in a large saucepan over medium heat. Cook 1 whole chicken carcass or 900g chicken bones and 2 cups (300g) mixed vegetable scraps for 5 minutes or until fragrant. Add 2.5 litres (10 cups) water, ½ teaspoon black peppercorns, 1 bay leaf and 1 bunch (30g) thyme or rosemary stalks. Bring to a gentle simmer over low heat; cook for 1½ hours or until fragrant. Cool completely; strain using a fine sieve. Store in the fridge for up to 5 days or freeze for up to 3 months.

TIP *Use the chicken carcass from the Classic Roast Chicken & Stuffing on page 24, or ask your butcher for bones.*

VEGETABLE STOCK

PREP + COOK TIME
1 HOUR
MAKES 6 CUPS

Heat 2 tablespoons olive oil in a large saucepan over medium heat. Cook 4 cups (600g) mixed vegetable scraps for 5 minutes or until fragrant. Add 2 litres (8 cups) water, ½ teaspoon black peppercorns, ⅓ cup (12g) dried mushrooms, 1 bay leaf, 1 bunch (30g) herb stalks and 2 teaspoons nutritional yeast (optional). Bring to a gentle simmer over low heat; cook for 45 minutes or until fragrant. Cool completely; strain using a fine sieve. Store in the fridge for up to 5 days or freeze for up to 3 months.

TIP *Compost your vegetable scraps after straining.*

PREP + COOK TIME 35 MINUTES **SERVES** 4

GREEN YOGHURT CURRY WITH SPICED PANEER

CHOOSE FROM KALE, CAVOLO NERO, SILVERBEET OR THE SOFTER SPINACH FOR THIS GREENS-PACKED CURRY. BE SURE TO RESERVE THE STEMS FOR THE WASTE-NOT RECIPE.

¼ cup (60ml) olive oil
400g can chickpeas, drained, rinsed (see swap ins)
200g paneer cheese, cut into 2cm cubes
1 tbsp garam masala
2 tsp ground cumin
1 medium onion (150g), sliced thinly
1 tbsp finely chopped ginger
2 cloves garlic, crushed
1 bunch coriander, leaves picked, roots and stems chopped coarsely
1 long red or green chilli, sliced thinly
1 bunch thick leafy greens (1kg), sliced thinly, stems reserved (see waste not)
1 cup (250ml) vegetable stock, warmed
1½ cups (420g) Greek yoghurt
basmati rice, naan and lemon wedges, to serve

1 Heat 2 tablespoons of the oil in a large frying pan over medium-high heat. Cook chickpeas, tossing, for 5 minutes or until starting to turn golden. Add paneer; cook, tossing, for 3 minutes or until paneer is golden. Add garam masala and cumin; cook, tossing, for 2 minutes or until fragrant. Transfer to a plate. Season to taste.

2 Wipe out frying pan. Heat remaining oil over medium-high heat. Cook onion, stirring, for 5 minutes or until softened. Add ginger, garlic, coriander roots and stems, and half the chilli; cook, stirring, for 1 minute or until fragrant. Add leafy greens; cook for 2 minutes or until wilted.

3 Stir stock and yoghurt into greens mixture until heated through; season to taste.

4 Top curry with paneer-chickpea mixture, coriander leaves and remaining chilli. Serve with rice, naan and lemon wedges.

SWAP INS *Instead of chickpeas, you could use any variety of canned beans.*

WASTE NOT *Use the reserved leafy greens stems to make Brown Butter Leek & Pea Linguine, page 59. Store, covered, in the fridge for up to 4 days.*

SAUCY

SWAP INS

✹ ✹ ✹

INSTEAD OF LINGUINE, YOU COULD USE WHICHEVER PASTA SHAPE YOU HAVE ON HAND. INSTEAD OF PARMESAN, YOU COULD USE CHEDDAR, PECORINO OR YOUR CHEESE OF CHOICE.

PREP + COOK TIME 30 MINUTES **SERVES** 4

BROWN BUTTER LEEK & PEA LINGUINE

THE GREEN LEAFY TIPS OF LEEKS ARE EDIBLE AND ADD A WELCOME TEXTURAL BITE; JUST BE SURE TO SLICE THEM EXTRA THIN, AS THEY HAVE A COARSE TEXTURE.

150g butter
2 large leeks (1kg), sliced thinly (see note above)
400g linguine (see swap ins)
2 tbsp olive oil
660g leftover thick leafy greens stems, sliced thinly (see tip)
4 cloves garlic, sliced thinly
½ cup (60g) frozen peas
½ cup (40g) grated parmesan (see swap ins)
1 lemon, rind grated finely, then juiced

1 Heat half the butter in a frying pan over medium heat. Cook half the leek, stirring occasionally, for 10 minutes or until golden and tender. Remove with a slotted spoon; drain on paper towel.

2 Meanwhile, cook pasta following packet directions. Reserve 1 cup (250ml) pasta water, then drain.

3 Heat oil and remaining butter in same pan over medium heat. Cook greens stems, remaining leek and the garlic for 8 minutes or until leek is just tender and butter is browned.

4 Add pasta, peas, parmesan and reserved pasta water to pan; cook, tossing, for 2 minutes or until pasta is well coated and peas are tender. Remove from heat. Add lemon rind and juice to taste; season.

5 Serve pasta topped with fried leek and sprinkled with freshly ground pepper.

TIP *We used Swiss chard stems, but you could use any leftover thick leafy greens stems, including silverbeet, kale and collard greens.*

ODDS & ENDS

ODDS & ENDS
ODDS & ENDS
ODDS & ENDS
ODDS & ENDS
ODDS & ENDS

PREP + COOK TIME 55 MINUTES **SERVES** 8 (AS A SIDE)

CRISP-CRUSHED HERBY POTATOES

THIS WORKS BEST WITH BABY (CHAT) POTATOES, BUT WHATEVER VARIETY YOU USE WILL BE DELICIOUS. LIGHTLY WHISKED EGG WHITES BRING AN EXTRA CRUNCH TO THESE ROAST POTATOES.

1.5kg potatoes, skin on
¼ cup (60ml) olive oil
2 egg whites
¼ cup rosemary leaves, chopped (see swap ins)
¼ cup thyme leaves, chopped (see swap ins)
2 tsp fine salt
1 tsp freshly ground pepper, plus extra to serve
⅔ cup (160g) sour cream
½ cup chives, chopped finely

1 Preheat oven to 200°C/180°C fan-forced.

2 Cook potatoes in a large saucepan of salted boiling water for 20 minutes or until tender. Drain then cool.

3 Place oil, egg whites, rosemary, thyme, the salt and pepper in a large bowl; whisk for 2 minutes or until thickened and foamy.

4 Using your hands, lightly crush the potatoes, then add to egg white mixture; toss to coat.

5 Place potatoes on an oven tray lined with baking paper. Roast for 25 minutes, opening the oven door briefly halfway through cooking to let out the steam (see tip), or until potatoes are golden and crispy.

6 Serve potatoes topped with sour cream and chives; season with extra pepper.

TIP *Opening the oven door briefly will let out steam, which will help the potatoes become extra crispy.*

SWAP INS

INSTEAD OF ROSEMARY AND THYME, YOU COULD USE OTHER WOODY HERBS, SUCH AS SAGE, OREGANO OR MARJORAM.

SWAP INS

INSTEAD OF CHEDDAR, YOU COULD USE GRUYÈRE, PARMESAN, HALOUMI, COMTE OR HAVARTI. INSTEAD OF THYME, YOU COULD USE ROSEMARY OR OREGANO.

PREP + COOK TIME 45 MINUTES (+ REFRIGERATION) **MAKES** 35

SESAME CHEESE BISCUITS

ADD YOUR OWN SPIN TO THESE BISCUITS BY ADDING YOUR FAVOURITE SPICE FROM YOUR SPICE DRAWER, SUCH AS FENNEL SEEDS, CHILLI FLAKES OR SMOKED PAPRIKA.

1¼ cups (185g) plain flour, sifted
125g cold butter, cubed
3 egg yolks
125g cheddar, grated coarsely (see swap ins)
1 tbsp thyme leaves, chopped finely (see swap ins)
½ tsp fine salt
½ cup (80g) mixed sesame seeds

1 Process flour, butter, egg yolks, cheddar, thyme and salt until the dough just comes together.

2 Turn the dough out onto a lightly floured work surface; roll and press into a 25cm long log.

3 Spread sesame seeds on a tray; roll and press the log in the sesame seeds to coat. Cover the dough on the tray and chill in the fridge for 30 minutes.

4 Meanwhile, preheat oven to 180°C/160°C fan-forced.

5 Slice the log into 5mm thick rounds; place on two lined oven trays, leaving 5cm between each round. Chill in the fridge for 20 minutes.

6 Bake biscuits for 25 minutes or until golden brown. Cool on tray.

PREP + COOK TIME 45 MINUTES **SERVES** 4 (OR 6 AS A SIDE)

FENNEL GRATIN

WE USED A MIX OF PARMESAN, CHEDDAR AND GRUYÈRE, BUT YOU CAN USE WHICHEVER MIX OF HARD CHEESES YOU HAVE ON HAND. IF YOU HAVE ANY SOFT CHEESES, CRUMBLE OVER THE GRATIN WHEN THE FOIL IS REMOVED.

---

1 cup (250ml) thickened cream
½ cup (125ml) vegetable stock or water
1⅔ cups (200g) hard cheese, grated (see note above)
½ tsp sweet paprika
2 large fennel bulbs (800g), sliced thickly lengthways, fronds reserved
2 tbsp olive oil
½ cup (50g) panko breadcrumbs (see swap ins)
2 tsp fennel seeds

1 Preheat oven to 200°C/180°C fan-forced. Combine cream, stock, cheese and paprika in a small bowl; season to taste.

2 Place fennel in a large baking dish and drizzle over the oil; toss to coat. Season. Pour cream mixture evenly over fennel.

3 Cover baking dish with foil. Bake for 10 minutes, then remove foil. Bake for a further 20 minutes or until fennel is tender and golden brown. Set aside to cool slightly.

4 Meanwhile, heat a medium frying pan over medium heat. Toast breadcrumbs and fennel seeds for 2 minutes or until golden brown; season to taste.

5 Serve gratin topped with toasted breadcrumbs and reserved fennel fronds.

SWAP INS *Instead of panko breadcrumbs, you could also use finely torn fresh or stale bread.*

SAUCY

SWAP INS

* * *

INSTEAD OF GRAPES, YOU COULD USE WHATEVER FRUIT IS IN SEASON, SUCH AS FIGS, STONE FRUIT, PEARS OR APPLES. WE USED RED WINE VINEGAR, BUT USE WHICHEVER VINEGAR YOU HAVE ON HAND.

PREP + COOK TIME 45 MINUTES **SERVES** 6

CHEESE SCONES WITH ROASTED GRAPES

WE USED A COMBINATION OF VINTAGE CHEDDAR AND GRUYÈRE, BUT ANY HARD CHEESE WILL WORK. THIS RECIPE CAN BE EASILY HALVED IF YOU HAVE LESS CHEESE ON HAND.

350g grapes (see swap ins)
2 tbsp caster sugar
2 tbsp vinegar (see swap ins)
3 cups (450g) self-raising flour, sifted, plus extra for dusting
2 tsp baking powder
1 tsp salt
½ tsp ground white pepper
120g butter, chilled, cubed
200g hard cheese, finely grated, plus 20g extra (see note above)
1 cup (250ml) milk, plus extra for brushing
mascarpone or crème fraîche, to serve

1 Preheat oven to 220°C/200°C fan-forced. Line an oven tray with baking paper and place in oven while preheating.

2 Combine grapes, sugar and vinegar in a medium baking tray. Roast for 35 minutes or until softened and syrupy.

3 Meanwhile, combine flour, baking powder, salt and white pepper in a medium bowl. Using your fingertips, rub in butter until resembling fine breadcrumbs.

4 Add cheese and milk to flour mixture. Using a butter knife, gently cut the mixture to bring the dough together; be careful not to overmix (see tip).

5 Turn the dough out onto a lightly floured surface; press into an 18cm x 30cm, 2½cm thick rectangle. Using a sharp knife, cut the dough into 12 even squares.

6 Place scones on preheated oven tray and brush tops with extra milk; scatter with extra grated cheese. Bake for 10 minutes or until light golden brown. Set aside to cool slightly.

7 Serve scones with mascarpone or crème fraîche and roasted grapes.

TIP *The cutting technique keeps the butter in small clumps, which helps the scone become extra flaky and tender.*

PREP + COOK TIME 1 HOUR 20 MINUTES **SERVES** 8

GREEK GREENS PIE

DUE TO THEIR SHORTER SHELF-LIFE AND PLASTIC PACKAGING, AIM TO BUY LEAFY GREENS BY THE BUNCH RATHER THAN BAGGED. IT'S MUCH CHEAPER TOO!

2 tbsp olive oil
1 large onion (300g), chopped finely
4 cloves garlic, crushed
350g leafy greens, chopped (see note above and swap ins), plus extra to serve
5 eggs
200g marinated fetta in oil, drained (see waste not)
¾ cup (180g) ricotta
2 tbsp finely chopped dill, stems and leaves, plus extra sprigs to serve (see swap ins)
¼ tsp ground nutmeg (optional)
12 sheets fillo pastry
125g butter, melted
2 tbsp mixed sesame seeds

1 Preheat oven to 180°C/160°C fan-forced. Lightly grease a 23cm springform cake pan.

2 Heat oil in a large frying pan over high heat. Cook onion and garlic, stirring, for 3 minutes or until softened. Add leafy greens; cook, stirring, for 3 minutes or until just wilted. Season to taste. Set aside to cool slightly.

3 Place eggs in a large bowl and whisk until combined. Add cooked greens, fetta, ricotta, dill and nutmeg; mash with a fork until combined.

4 Place 1 fillo sheet on a clean surface (see tip); lightly brush with butter, then top with another fillo sheet. Repeat layering process with 2 more fillo sheets. Place layered fillo into cake pan, allowing edges to overhang. Repeat the layering and brushing process with another 4 fillo sheets. Place second layered fillo in the pan in the opposite direction, allowing edges to overhang.

5 Add greens mixture to pastry case. Brush any overhanging fillo with butter, then fold over greens mixture to cover. Repeat layering process with remaining fillo sheets; scrunch and place on top of the pie. Sprinkle over sesame seeds.

6 Bake pie for 45 minutes or until golden. Cool in the pan for 5 minutes.

7 Top pie with extra dill sprigs. Serve with extra leafy greens.

TIP *While brushing fillo with butter, keep remaining fillo covered with a clean tea towel to prevent drying out.*

WASTE NOT *Keep the marinated fetta oil for dressings and sauces. Store any leftover pie, covered, in the fridge for up to 3 days.*

SWAP INS

* * *

FOR LEAFY GREENS, YOU COULD USE SPINACH, KALE, CABBAGE, SILVERBEET OR MIXED LEAVES. INSTEAD OF DILL, YOU COULD USE PARSLEY, MINT OR BASIL.

PREP + COOK TIME 35 MINUTES **SERVES** 4 (AS A SIDE)

CREAMY BRAISED GREENS WITH PANCETTA

SERVE WARM AS A SIDE OR AS AN ACCOMPANIMENT TO YOUR CHOICE OF PROTEIN. WE'VE USED 2 QUARTERED COS LETTUCES, BUT USE WHICHEVER LEAFY GREENS YOU HAVE ON HAND.

20g butter
1 medium leek (350g), stem and top, sliced thinly (see tips)
3 cloves garlic, crushed
100g pancetta, diced (see swap ins)
2 tsp plain flour
½ cup (125ml) chicken or vegetable stock
350g leafy greens (see note above)
150g sugar snap peas, halved lengthways
¾ cup (180g) crème fraîche (see swap ins)
½ cup dill sprigs (see swap ins)
croûtons and lemon wedges, to serve

1 Melt butter in a large, deep frying pan over medium heat. Cook leek for 6 minutes, stirring, or until softened. Add garlic and pancetta; cook for 5 minutes or until pancetta is golden.

2 Increase heat to high. Add flour to pan and cook, stirring, for 1 minute or until well combined. Add stock and stir to combine; bring to the boil. Add leafy greens (see tips). Cook for 2 minutes or until mixture is slightly reduced.

3 Stir in sugar snap peas and crème fraîche until combined; cook, stirring occasionally, for 2 minutes or until peas are just tender. Season to taste.

4 Top greens with dill and season with freshly ground pepper. Serve with croûtons and lemon wedges.

TIPS *Slice the leek top extra thin, as it has a coarser texture to the stem. If using soft greens, such as spinach, stir in with the peas and crème fraîche in step 3 instead.*

SWAP INS *Instead of pancetta, you could use bacon or prosciutto. Instead of crème fraîche, you could use sour cream or Greek yoghurt. Instead of dill, you could use parsley, mint, chives or basil.*

START A WORM FARM OR COMPOST

When you put your food scraps into a worm farm or compost, they break down and turn into a nutrient-rich resource that you can use in your garden or pot plants. This helps to create healthy soil to grow more healthy food to eat.

Healthy soil is like a healthy gut. Everything works better when it's all in balance.

Worms are the most practical and useful pets you can have. They clean up after you!

To make sure a worm farm can thrive and do its job, you'll need to feed and care for the worms like they are your pets. In fact, they are much more than that – they are your waste disposal unit and a super simple way to give your garden or pot plants a healthy boost.

When you start a worm farm or compost, you are creating a living ecosystem. In a compost or worm farm, there's an incredible amount of biological activity happening 24 hours a day. Tiny microbes do most of the work in breaking down organic materials, with a helping hand from our insects and worms.

Goldfish are often our go-to first pet for children, but worm farms can teach them so much more. A worm farm will get them outside and involved in the garden, and by helping, children will learn about the seasons, food, nutrition and our interconnectedness with nature.

And so can you. This all helps to deepen our understanding of the natural world around us. Even the tiniest creatures have a big job to do. We are interdependent on everything around us.

HOW TO

There are several types of worm farms and ways to compost. For example:

Stacked worm farm
These are stand-alone plastic worm farms with several layers. They are good for small spaces and balconies.

In-garden worm farm
These are worm farms that sit in a garden bed. The worms move freely in and out of the worm farm.

In-garden worm tube
These are small tubes which can be placed in a large pot or garden bed. They are a type of in-garden worm farm, just on a small scale.

Compost bin
These are containers that sit on the ground. They are great for backyards.

Compost tumbler
These are a drum on a stand and need to be turned regularly. They are good for backyards or a patio.

Bokashi bin
These are a great option if you don't have much space. This is a small bucket system that relies on a fermentation process. A special form of bran is added to break down the food.

TOP TIPS TO REMEMBER

When deciding where to put your compost or worm farm, choose a spot that's out of the hot sun. Worms are living creatures and need the right conditions to thrive and be able to do their job.

* * *

Find out what you can and can't put in your compost, worm farm or Bokashi bin. When it comes to worms, there are specific foods that should be avoided like onions and citrus.

* * *

Both compost and worm farms work best when they have a good mix of 'green' materials like food scraps and 'brown' materials like shredded paper and dry leaves. It should feel moist but not wet. If your compost or worm farm is too wet or smells, add more brown material.

You can put the nutrient-rich material from your compost, worm farm or Bokashi bin back into the garden. Remember that Bokashi waste needs to be buried in the garden. Follow the instructions carefully.

You can use the liquid from your worm farm or Bokashi bin as an amazing fertiliser. You'll never need to buy compost or fertilisers again!

* * *

As the saying goes, from little things big things grow.

PREP + COOK TIME 50 MINUTES **MAKES** 10

CHEAT'S RUM BABA

A DENSE AND CHEWY BREAD, SUCH AS SOURDOUGH, IS PREFERABLE FOR THIS RECIPE, ALTHOUGH ANY BREAD WILL BE DELICIOUS. THESE CAN BE SERVED EITHER HOT OR CHILLED.

3 eggs
1 cup (250ml) pouring cream
1½ tbsp rum (see swap ins)
60g butter, melted
½ cup (110g) caster sugar
1 tsp vanilla
2 tsp finely grated orange rind
1 tsp baking powder
300g sliced leftover bread, crusts on, cut into 2cm squares (see note above)
½ cup (65g) dried cranberries
whipped cream, to serve

SYRUP

1 cup (220g) caster sugar
½ cup (125ml) rum (see swap ins)
¼ tsp fine salt
6 wide orange rind strips
2 tsp finely grated orange rind
⅓ cup (80ml) orange juice

1 Preheat oven to 200°C/180°C fan-forced. Grease 10 holes of a 12-hole (¾-cup/180ml) Texas muffin pan; line the base of each with a round of baking paper.

2 Place eggs, cream, rum, butter, sugar, vanilla, orange rind and baking powder in a large bowl; whisk until well combined. Add bread and massage with your hands until softened.

3 Blend or process bread mixture for 1 minute or until smooth and batter-like; transfer to a large jug. Add cranberries and gently stir to combine.

4 Pour ⅓ cup (80ml) of the batter into each lined muffin hole. Bake for 25 minutes or until golden brown. Cool in the pan for 10 minutes before transferring babas to a wire rack.

5 Meanwhile, make the syrup: Place sugar and 2 cups (500ml) water in a medium saucepan. Bring to the boil over medium-high heat. Reduce heat to medium. Simmer for 10 minutes or until reduced by a third. Add rum, salt, orange rinds and juice; stir to combine. Set aside to cool for 5 minutes.

6 Working in batches, place the babas in the syrup for 2 minutes, turning to coat; transfer to a plate.

7 Serve rum babas topped with whipped cream and orange rind from syrup; drizzle with remaining syrup.

SWAP INS *Instead of rum, you could use brandy or any brown sweet spirit.*

TASTY

SWAP INS

WE USED SOURDOUGH, BUT USE WHICHEVER BREAD YOU HAVE ON HAND.

PREP + COOK TIME 1 HOUR **SERVES** 4

ITALIAN SAVOURY BREAD PUDDING

THIS SAVOURY BREAD PUDDING COMBINES CUSTARDY BREAD SLICES WITH OOZY MOZZARELLA. YOU COULD ALSO USE GRUYÈRE, CHEDDAR OR BRIE INSTEAD OF MOZZARELLA.

¼ cup (60ml) olive oil, plus 2 tbsp extra
3 cloves garlic, crushed
3 anchovy fillets
2 tsp chilli flakes, plus extra to serve
2 large shallots (60g), sliced thinly
1 bunch silverbeet (750g), stalks chopped finely, leaves chopped coarsely
2 eggs
1½ cups (375ml) pouring cream
½ tsp ground nutmeg
½ loaf of bread (350g), torn into large chunks (see swap ins)
400g mozzarella, sliced (see note above)
1 cup (80g) finely grated parmesan

1 Preheat oven to 200°C/180°C fan-forced. Grease a deep 22cm x 30cm baking dish with oil.

2 Heat the oil in a large frying pan over medium-high heat. Cook garlic, anchovy and chilli flakes for 1 minute or until fragrant. Add shallots and silverbeet stalks; cook, stirring, for 3 minutes or until shallots are tender. Add silverbeet leaves; cook for 2 minutes or until just starting to wilt. Remove from heat.

3 Place eggs, cream and nutmeg in a large jug; whisk until well combined. Season to taste. Arrange bread in the baking dish; evenly pour over the egg mixture.

4 Place ⅔ cup of the silverbeet mixture and a piece of mozzarella between each bread piece; fill any gaps with remaining silverbeet mixture. Sprinkle over parmesan and drizzle over extra oil. Bake for 30 minutes or until golden brown and set.

5 Serve bread pudding sprinkled with extra chilli flakes.

PREP + COOK TIME 1 HOUR (+ STANDING) **SERVES** 4

CARROT & POTATO RÖSTI

SERVE RÖSTI WITH YOUR FAVOURITE CONDIMENTS AND WHICHEVER LEAFY GREENS AND FRESH HERBS YOU HAVE ON HAND. YOU WILL NEED AN OVENPROOF FRYING PAN FOR THIS RECIPE.

600g potatoes (see swap ins)
600g carrots
2 green onions, chopped finely (see swap ins)
2 tbsp lemon thyme leaves
1 small bunch parsley, leaves picked, stems chopped finely
4 egg whites, beaten lightly (see waste not)
¼ cup (35g) cornflour
1 tbsp olive oil
100g butter, chopped
whipped goat's cheese, sliced avocado and rocket leaves, to serve (see note above)

1 Preheat oven to 200°C/180°C fan-forced. Scrub and coarsely grate potatoes and carrots.

2 Rinse potato and carrot in a large bowl of cold water; drain then squeeze out excess water. Spread out on paper towel and pat dry.

3 Combine grated potato and carrot, the green onion, lemon thyme, parsley stems, egg white and cornflour in a large bowl; season well.

4 Heat oil and butter in a 26cm ovenproof frying pan over medium heat; add potato-carrot mixture and press firmly to flatten. Cook for 5 minutes or until base is lightly browned.

5 Transfer pan to oven. Roast rösti for 25 minutes, then invert onto a lined oven tray.

6 Preheat oven grill to high. Grill rösti for 10 minutes or until golden brown.

7 To serve, spread goat's cheese over rösti; top with parsley leaves, avocado and rocket. Season with freshly ground pepper.

SWAP INS *Instead of potatoes, you could also use sweet potatoes. Swap green onions with regular onions or shallots.*

WASTE NOT

* * *

RESERVE THE EGG YOLKS TO MAKE THE SESAME CHEESE BISCUITS, PAGE 65.

PREP + COOK TIME 45 MINUTES **SERVES** 4

ROAST CARROT & LENTILS WITH HARISSA

HARISSA IS A SPICED TOMATO AND CAPSICUM PASTE FROM TUNISIA. YOU COULD ALSO USE A CHILLI PASTE OR HOT SAUCE, ADJUSTING THE QUANTITY IN THE DRESSING TO TASTE.

12 carrots (1kg), halved lengthways
2 red onions, cut into 1cm wedges
2 cloves garlic, skin on
1½ tbsp caraway seeds (see swap ins)
¼ cup (60ml) olive oil
¼ cup (50g) French-style green lentils (see swap ins)
2 tsp harissa paste (see note above)
1 tsp honey
2 tsp vinegar (see swap ins)
⅓ cup (100g) Greek yoghurt
¼ cup coriander, stems and leaves, chopped coarsely
¼ cup (25g) toasted walnuts, chopped coarsely (see swap ins)
toasted pitta bread, to serve

1 Preheat oven to 220°C/200°C fan-forced.

2 Place carrots, onions and garlic on a lined oven tray; sprinkle over caraway seeds and drizzle with half the oil. Season to taste. Roast for 30 minutes or until vegetables are golden and tender. Peel the garlic; discard skin.

3 Meanwhile, cook lentils in a medium saucepan of boiling water for 18 minutes or until tender. Drain then rinse under cold water; return to pan.

4 Combine harissa, honey, vinegar, roasted garlic and remaining oil in a small bowl; season to taste.

5 To serve, spread yoghurt over the base of bowls and drizzle with half the harissa dressing; top with lentils and roasted carrots and onions. Drizzle over remaining dressing; top with coriander and walnuts. Serve with toasted pitta bread.

SWAP INS *Instead of caraway seeds, you could use fennel seeds. Swap dried lentils with canned lentils or any other canned legume. We've used red wine vinegar, but use whichever vinegar you have on hand. Instead of walnuts, you could use pistachios, pine nuts or almonds.*

ZERO WASTE LIVING

Despite our best intentions, in our busy lives it's common that a large amount of waste happens in our kitchens, from excess packaging to spoilage. This can be avoided with smart food planning and storage. Swap single-use and plastic with the items below.

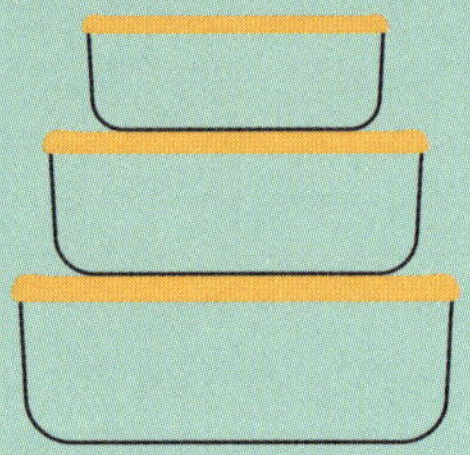

CONTAINERS

Place leftover food and other produce in reusable glass or stainless-steel airtight containers for longer storage.

BEESWAX WRAPS

Cover leftovers with stretchy silicone lids or beeswax wraps, which mould to the shape of whatever you are covering.

GLASS JARS

Store leafy greens in a jar of water in the fridge. Recycled jars are also great for storing sauces, dressings, oils and other liquids.

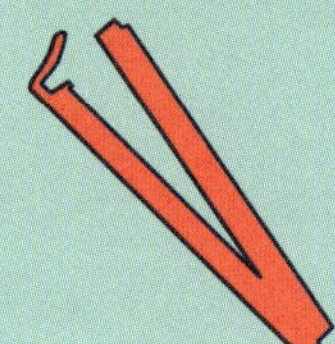

FOOD CLIPS

Use food clips to seal open packets to store in your pantry or the refrigerator.

REDUCE YOUR FOOTPRINT

While it's good to try and reduce the waste in your home, it's harder to do so when you're eating out. A few little changes go a long way, like avoiding single-use.

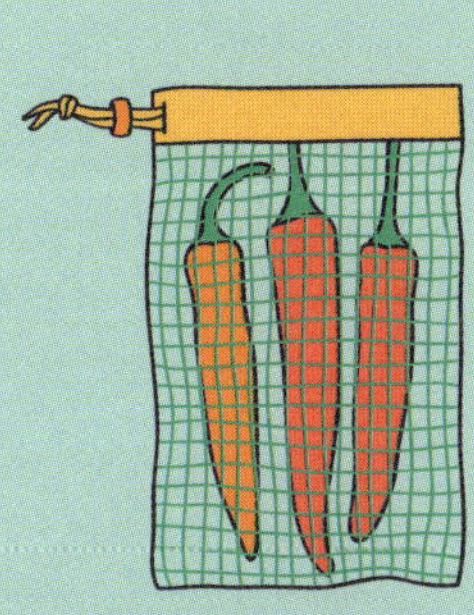

PRODUCE BAGS

Use reusable drawstring bags when buying and storing produce, especially those small loose vegetables such as green beans.

TRAVEL CUTLERY

Take a set of reusable cutlery with you the next time you go on a picnic or have to eat on-the-go.

COFFEE MUG

Single-use paper coffee cups are not recyclable, as they have a layer of plastic inside the cup to prevent leaks.

REUSABLE STRAWS

Plastic straws create long-lasting pollution and are easy for sea life to ingest. Swap to a more eco-friendly reusable type.

PREP + COOK TIME 45 MINUTES **MAKES** 1

NO-KNEAD MUSHROOM PIZZA

GET CREATIVE AND MAKE THIS PIZZA YOUR OWN BY SPREADING AND SPRINKLING YOUR FAVOURITE TOPPINGS ON THIS NO-KNEAD DOUGH BASE.

100g thick leafy greens, stems and leaves, chopped coarsely (see swap ins)
⅓ cup (80ml) olive oil, plus extra to drizzle
1 tsp salt flakes
450g mixed mushrooms, halved if large
2 tbsp thyme leaves (see swap ins)
4 cloves garlic, crushed
½ cup (120g) ricotta
200g mozzarella, shredded coarsely (see swap ins)
1½ cups (225g) self-raising flour
1 cup (280g) Greek yoghurt
shaved parmesan, to serve (optional)

1 Preheat oven to 220°C/200°C fan-forced.

2 Place the thick leafy green leaves (not the stems) in a large bowl and add 1 tablespoon of the oil and half the salt; rub until slightly softened. Place leaves on a lined oven tray. Roast, tossing halfway through cooking, for 10 minutes or until crisp.

3 Meanwhile, heat 2 tablespoons of the oil in a large frying pan over high heat. Cook mushrooms and leafy green stems, stirring, for 4 minutes or until golden. Add thyme and half the garlic; cook for 1 minute or until fragrant. Season to taste.

4 Combine ricotta, mozzarella, remaining oil and remaining garlic in a small bowl; season to taste.

5 Place flour, remaining salt and the yoghurt in a medium bowl; mix to make a soft dough. Turn dough out onto a large sheet of baking paper; roll out into a 34cm round.

6 Transfer dough on baking paper to an oven tray; spread over cheese mixture. Bake for 20 minutes or until base is browned and crisp.

7 Serve pizza topped with mushroom mixture, roasted greens and parmesan; season with freshly ground pepper and drizzle with extra olive oil.

SWAP INS

THICK LEAFY GREENS COULD BE KALE, CAVOLO NERO, SWISS CHARD OR SILVERBEET; WE'VE USED CAVOLO NERO. SWAP THYME WITH ROSEMARY, OREGANO OR DRIED THYME. INSTEAD OF MOZZARELLA, YOU COULD ALSO USE ANY MELTING CHEESE.

SWAP INS

INSTEAD OF PISTACHIOS, YOU COULD USE WALNUTS, ALMONDS, PECANS OR MACADAMIAS.

PREP + COOK TIME 20 MINUTES **SERVES** 4

YOGHURT POTS WITH CITRUS SALSA

YOU COULD ALSO USE OTHER CITRUS, SUCH AS MANDARINS, GRAPEFRUITS OR POMELO. DEPENDING ON THE SEASON, YOU COULD ALSO TRY BERRIES, GRAPES OR RIPE STONE FRUIT.

1 tsp vanilla bean paste
½ cup (110g) caster sugar
1 large lemon (150g), rind removed in wide strips, then juiced
2 blood oranges (360g), peeled, sliced (see note above)
2 medium oranges (480g), peeled, sliced (see note above)
3 cups (840g) Greek yoghurt
¼ cup (35g) toasted pistachios, chopped (see swap ins)

1 Place vanilla, sugar, lemon rind and ½ cup (125ml) water in a small saucepan; bring to the boil. Reduce heat. Simmer for 6 minutes or until syrup is slightly thickened. Cool.

2 Stir lemon juice into syrup; add orange slices and toss to coat.

3 Spoon yoghurt into four 1¼-cups (310ml) serving glasses; top with citrus salsa.

4 Serve sprinkled with pistachios.

WASTE NOT *Keep any remaining citrus and peels for the Citrus Tea Jam, page 41. Store, covered, in the fridge for up to 4 days.*

PREP + COOK TIME 35 MINUTES **SERVES** 4

GRILLED VEGIE BRUSCHETTA WITH NUT SPREAD

USE THIS SAVOURY NUT SPREAD TO ELEVATE SANDWICHES AND SAUCES. WE'VE USED A MIX OF HAZELNUTS, WALNUTS AND ALMONDS FOR THIS RECIPE, BUT USE WHATEVER ASSORTMENT YOU HAVE ON HAND.

---

1 medium eggplant (300g) (see swap ins)
1 large zucchini (150g) (see swap ins)
1 medium capsicum (200g) (see swap ins)
140ml olive oil, plus extra to drizzle
300g loaf of bread
1½ tbsp balsamic vinegar
1 tbsp honey
¾ cup (100g) roasted mixed nuts and seeds, chopped coarsely (see note above and waste not)
3 cloves garlic, crushed
2 tbsp lemon juice
2 tsp vinegar (see swap ins)
¼ cup (20g) grated parmesan
rocket leaves, to serve

1 Preheat a grill plate or barbecue. Slice eggplant and zucchini lengthways into thin strips. Cut capsicum into quarters and remove the seeds. Brush vegetables on both sides with ¼ cup (60ml) of the oil; season to taste.

2 Cut ends off bread loaf and reserve for the nut spread; you will need about 70g. Slice remaining bread into eight even pieces; brush with 1 tablespoon of the oil.

3 Cook vegetables on the grill plate or barbecue for 3 minutes each side or until just tender and grill marks appear. Combine balsamic vinegar and honey in a medium bowl; add grilled vegetables and toss to coat.

4 Cook bread slices on grill plate or barbecue for 2 minutes each side or until grill marks appear.

5 Blend or process ½ cup (70g) of the nut and seed mix until fine crumbs form. Add reserved bread and blend or process to fine crumbs. Add garlic, lemon juice, vinegar, remaining oil, the parmesan and ¾ cup (180ml) water; process until well combined. Season to taste.

6 Slice grilled vegetables. Spread nut spread over bread slices; top with vegetables, rocket and remaining nut and seed mix. Finish with a drizzle of extra olive oil.

SWAP INS *Pick your vegetables for grilling based on seasonal availability; this could include vine-ripened tomatoes, asparagus, broccolini, green beans or mushrooms. We've used red wine vinegar, but use whichever vinegar you have on hand.*

WASTE NOT

IF SEALED PROPERLY, NUTS CAN LAST FOR UP TO 3 MONTHS IN A DARK, DRY PLACE, AND FOR EVEN LONGER IN THE FRIDGE OR FREEZER.

SWAP INS

✱ ✱ ✱

INSTEAD OF OATS, PUFFED RICE AND ALL-BRAN FLAKES, YOU COULD USE WHICHEVER UNSWEETENED CEREAL YOU HAVE ON HAND.

PREP + COOK TIME 30 MINUTES **MAKES** 5 CUPS

SAVOURY PANTRY MUESLI

PERFECT FOR HALF-USED PANTRY PACKETS, ENJOY THIS SALTY SNACK ON ITS OWN OR SPRINKLE OVER SALADS, DIPS AND VEGETABLES. STORE IN A JAR OR AIRTIGHT CONTAINER FOR UP TO 1 MONTH.

1 cup (90g) rolled oats (see swap ins)
¾ cup (150g) mixed seeds
1½ cups (210g) mixed nuts, chopped coarsely
1 cup (25g) puffed rice (see swap ins)
1 cup (45g) All-Bran flakes (see swap ins)
2 packets (10g) roasted seaweed, torn coarsely (optional)
½ tsp salt flakes
⅓ cup (80ml) soy sauce
⅓ cup (80ml) olive oil
2 tbsp sesame oil
1 tbsp maple syrup
½ tsp chilli flakes

1 Preheat oven to 180°C/160°C fan-forced.

2 Combine oats, seeds, nuts, puffed rice, bran flakes, seaweed and salt in a large bowl.

3 Place soy sauce, oils, maple syrup and chilli flakes in a medium jug; whisk until well combined. Pour oil mixture over cereal mixture; stir until well coated.

4 Spread muesli over a lined oven tray. Bake for 20 minutes, stirring halfway through cooking, or until golden brown and crisp. Set aside to cool completely.

REGROW IT!

Free food is at your fingertips. It takes just one tiny seed from an old chilli or pumpkin and you could get a year's worth of abundant produce. Didn't get to eat the potatoes in time? Pop them into a pot of soil or plant them in your garden. Have a pineapple top? Don't throw it out; it will grow just about anywhere.

Enjoy the process of seeing what you can regrow from your vegetable, fruit and herb scraps. Try on your windowsill or plant straight into the garden – no green thumb is required. With just a little time and energy, there are many secrets to be discovered in your kitchen and garden.

SEEDS TO COLLECT

chilli, capsicum, pumpkin, avocado, mango, watermelon

HOW TO GROW

Reserve any seeds and plant them right away. Put them in a pot of soil on the kitchen ledge but not in direct sunlight; water regularly. You can also germinate seeds first by wrapping them in damp paper towel and placing in a zip-lock bag.

HERBS TO LOVE

peppermint, spearmint, common mint, basil, tulsi (holy basil), stevia, sage, lemon balm, lemon verbena, stinging nettles (use gloves as this plant has a fiery sting)

HOW TO GROW

Place a herb cutting in a jar of water; stand in a sunny spot, changing the water regularly. After roots have appeared, plant them in a pot of soil or in the garden. Many herb leaves can also be made into healing teas or can be used to make topical creams and lotions. Bees and other beneficial pollinator insects also love flowering herbs, so they're wonderful to have in your garden.

ROOTS & CUTTINGS TO GROW

onion, green onion, pineapple, oregano, thyme, ginger, turmeric

HOW TO GROW

Place roots in a jar of water for a few days or until you see some root growth, or plant directly into the soil in either a pot or the garden. Once the root is in the ground watch it, as some plants need more water than others. Anything freshly planted needs a good drink to start.

HERBY SAUCES

THESE TWO SAUCES ARE A GREAT WAY TO USE UP ANY HERBS YOU MAY HAVE IN YOUR FRIDGE. USE PESTO SPOONED OVER GRILLED MEATS OR FISH, TOSSED THROUGH PASTA OR AS A BASE FOR SANDWICHES. SALSA VERDE PAIRS WELL WITH BARBECUED MEATS, FISH AND VEGETABLES; YOU COULD ALSO STIR IT THROUGH STOCKS AND SAUCES.

PESTO

PREP TIME 10 MINUTES
MAKES 1 CUP

Blend or process ½ cup toasted pine nuts (see swap ins), 2½ cups (firmly packed) basil and parsley leaves and stems (see swap ins), ¼ cup finely grated parmesan, 1 peeled clove garlic, 2 teaspoons finely grated lemon rind, 2 teaspoons lemon juice and ½ cup (125ml) olive oil until smooth; season to taste.

SWAP INS *Instead of pine nuts, you could use almonds, cashews or walnuts. If you don't have any nuts, make an equally delicious French sauce called pistou by omitting the nuts and adding more cheese to taste. Instead of basil, you could use a combination of any soft herb.*

STORING *Store in a jar, covered in a thin layer of olive oil, in the fridge for up to 1 week, or freeze in ice-cube trays, then store cubes in sealed bags in the freezer for up to 6 months.*

SALSA VERDE

PREP TIME 10 MINUTES
MAKES ¾ CUP

Blend or process 2½ cups (firmly packed) herb leaves and stems (see swap ins), 1 tablespoon drained capers (see swap ins), 1 peeled clove garlic, 1 teaspoon caster sugar, ½ cup (125ml) olive oil and 1½ tablespoons white wine vinegar until well combined; season to taste.

SWAP INS *You could use a combination of mint, basil and parsley. Instead of capers, you could use olives or gherkins.*

STORING *Store in a jar, covered in a thin layer of olive oil, in the fridge for up to 3 days, or freeze in ice-cube trays, then store cubes in sealed bags in the freezer for up to 6 months.*

SAUCY

HERB DRESSING & PASTE

BOTH THESE ASIAN-INSPIRED RECIPES ARE GREAT TO HAVE IN YOUR FRIDGE TO LIVEN UP MEAL TIMES. THE ASIAN DIPPING DRESSING GOES WELL WITH A VARIETY OF MEATS OR SEAFOOD, WHILE THE CURRY PASTE CAN BE USED WITH A MIX OF PROTEINS AND VEGETABLES. COOK PASTE UNTIL FRAGRANT, STIR THROUGH A 400ML CAN OF COCONUT MILK OR CREAM, THEN SIMMER UNTIL REDUCED.

ASIAN DIPPING DRESSING

PREP TIME 10 MINUTES
MAKES 1 CUP

Blend or process 3 peeled cloves garlic, 3 seeded long red chillies, ½ cup (firmly packed) coriander (see tips), 2 tablespoons fish sauce, 1 tablespoon caster sugar, 3 halved shallots (see swap ins) and ¼ cup (60ml) lime juice until coarsely chopped; season to taste.

TIPS *Soak coriander in cold water before use to remove dirt and grit from its roots and between its stems. Use leftover coriander leaves, roots and stems in a green sauce, such as salsa verde or zhoug.*

SWAP INS *Instead of shallots, you could also use half an onion or 2 green onions.*

STORING *Store in a jar in the fridge for up to 4 days.*

CURRY PASTE

PREP TIME 15 MINUTES
MAKES 1½ CUPS

Blend or process 1½ cups firmly packed herbs (see tips), 4 peeled cloves garlic, ¼ cup (40g) chopped ginger, 1 seeded long green chilli, 150g chopped leafy greens (see tips), ½ cup (125ml) oil (see tips), 1 tablespoon garam masala, 1 teaspoon ground turmeric, 2 teaspoons toasted cumin seeds (see swap ins) and 1 teaspoon salt flakes until a smooth paste forms; season to taste.

TIPS *Herbs that can be used are coriander (stems and roots) and mint. Leafy greens include buk choy, gai lan, kale or spinach. Use a neutral oil, such as vegetable, sunflower, grapeseed, peanut or rice bran.*

SWAP INS *You could use a blend of spices, including fennel seeds, mustard seeds, coriander seeds, black peppercorns and ground cinnamon.*

STORING *Store in a jar in the fridge for up to 4 days, or freeze in ice-cube trays, then store cubes in sealed bags in the freezer for up to 6 months.*

PREP + COOK TIME 1 HOUR **SERVES** 4

CRISPY PANCETTA CHICKPEA PASTA

USE A COMBINATION OF WHICHEVER SHORT PASTA YOU HAVE IN YOUR PANTRY, SUCH AS PENNE OR FUSILLI.

2 tbsp olive oil
100g pancetta, chopped (see swap ins)
1 large onion (200g), chopped
2 celery stalks (300g), sliced thinly
1½ tsp fennel seeds
½–1 tsp chilli flakes
3 cloves garlic, crushed
1 tbsp rosemary leaves, chopped
2 tbsp tomato paste
⅔ cup (160ml) dry white wine
400g can cherry tomatoes
2 x 400g cans chickpeas, drained, rinsed (see swap ins)
2 cups (500ml) chicken or vegetable stock
1 parmesan rind (30g), (optional)
400g short pasta
1⅓ cups (100g) finely grated parmesan

CRISPY PANCETTA CHICKPEAS

400g can chickpeas, drained, rinsed (see swap ins)
75g pancetta, chopped (see swap ins)
2 tbsp rosemary leaves
1 clove garlic, crushed
2 tbsp olive oil

1 Preheat oven to 220°C/200°C fan-forced.

2 Heat oil in a large frying pan over medium-high heat. Cook pancetta, stirring, for 5 minutes or until golden. Add onion, celery, fennel seeds and chilli flakes; cook, stirring, for 5 minutes until vegetables are softened. Add garlic, rosemary and tomato paste; cook, stirring, for 2 minutes or until fragrant.

3 Add wine to pan and bring to the boil; cook for 2 minutes or until reduced by half. Add tomatoes, chickpeas, stock and parmesan rind; bring to the boil. Reduce heat to low-medium. Simmer for 30 minutes until reduced. Discard parmesan rind.

4 Meanwhile, make the crispy pancetta chickpeas: Combine ingredients on a lined oven tray. Roast for 20 minutes until golden and crisp; season.

5 Cook pasta following packet directions. Reserve ½ cup (125ml) pasta water, then drain.

6 Add pasta, grated parmesan and reserved pasta water to pancetta sauce; toss for 2 minutes or until the pasta is well coated and the sauce is glossy. Season to taste.

7 Serve pasta seasoned with freshly ground pepper and topped with crispy pancetta chickpeas.

SWAP INS *Instead of pancetta, you could use bacon or speck. Swap chickpeas with whichever variety of beans you have on hand.*

SWAP INS

WE USED SHERRY VINEGAR, BUT USE WHICHEVER VINEGAR YOU HAVE ON HAND. INSTEAD OF PARSLEY, YOU COULD USE ANY OTHER SOFT HERB. INSTEAD OF ALMONDS, YOU COULD USE WALNUTS, PISTACHIOS, OR PINE NUTS.

PREP + COOK TIME 40 MINUTES **SERVES** 4

SMOKY CAPSICUM PASTA

KEEP THIS DISH VEGAN OR SERVE WITH GRATED CHEESE, IF YOU LIKE.

40g miso paste
2 tbsp tomato paste
1 vegetable stock cube, crumbled
⅓ cup (80ml) olive oil
3 cloves garlic, peeled
1 tsp smoked paprika
½ tsp chilli flakes (optional)
340g jarred roasted capsicums, drained
400g can chopped tomatoes
2 tsp vinegar (see swap ins)
400g long pasta of your choice

LEMON ALMOND SALSA
½ lemon, including rind, chopped finely (see waste not)
¼ cup parsley, chopped coarsely (see swap ins)
⅓ cup (80ml) olive oil
¼ cup (40g) roasted almonds, chopped coarsely (see swap ins)

1 Place miso, tomato paste, stock cube and 1 cup (250ml) boiling water in a heatproof jug or bowl; whisk until combined.

2 Heat oil in a large frying pan over medium-high heat. Cook garlic, paprika and chilli flakes for 2 minutes until fragrant. Add half the capsicums, the tomatoes and miso stock mixture; bring to the boil. Reduce heat to medium. Simmer, stirring occasionally, for 15 minutes or until sauce is reduced. Remove from heat. Stir in vinegar.

3 Blend or process capsicum sauce until smooth; season to taste. Return sauce to pan.

4 Cook pasta following packet directions. Reserve ¾ cup (180ml) pasta water, then drain.

5 Meanwhile, make the lemon almond salsa: Combine ingredients in a medium bowl. Season to taste.

6 Thinly slice remaining capsicums. Heat capsicum sauce over medium-high heat. Add pasta, sliced capsicum and reserved pasta water; toss for 2 minutes or until the pasta is well coated and the sauce is glossy. Season to taste.

7 Serve pasta topped with lemon almond salsa and seasoned with freshly ground pepper.

WASTE NOT *Keep any remaining lemon to make the Citrus Tea Jam, page 41. Store, covered, in the fridge for up to 4 days.*

CHUTNEY & RELISH

TRANSFORM LEFTOVERS, OFFCUTS OR IMPERFECT FRUIT AND VEGETABLES INTO THESE PRESERVES. USE WHICHEVER VEGETABLE TRIMMINGS YOU HAVE ON HAND FOR THE PICCALILLI, AND SWAP THE PLUMS AND RHUBARB FOR ANY FRUIT YOU LIKE TO MAKE A VARIATION OF THE CHUTNEY.

VEGIE ENDS PICCALILLI

PREP + COOK TIME 30 MINUTES (+ STANDING) **MAKES** 5 CUPS

Thinly slice 1 onion and 1 long red chilli. Combine onion, chilli, 3¼ cups (510g) thinly sliced mixed vegetable trimmings (see tip) and 2 teaspoons fine salt in a large bowl. Set aside for at least 4 hours or overnight. Drain and rinse vegetables. Combine 2 tablespoons cornflour, 1 tablespoon mustard seeds, 1 tablespoon mustard powder, 1 teaspoon coriander seeds, 1 teaspoon cumin seeds, 1 teaspoon ground turmeric and ¼ cup (60ml) white wine vinegar in a small bowl. Heat ½ cup (110g) caster sugar and an extra 1 cup (250ml) white wine vinegar in a large saucepan over medium heat for 2 minutes or until sugar dissolves. Add spice paste and cook, stirring, for 1 minute or until thickened. Add drained vegetables and cook for 1 minute. Transfer to a sterilised jar (see page 160). Store for at least 1 month before consuming.

TIP *You could use a mix of carrot, celery, zucchini, green bean or capsicum trimmings, and cauliflower or broccoli stems and leaves.*

RHUBARB, HARISSA & PLUM CHUTNEY

PREP + COOK TIME 1 HOUR **MAKES** 6 CUPS

Finely chop 1 long red chilli, 1 onion and a 3cm piece of fresh ginger (30g). Quarter 6 plums (675g) and place in a large saucepan. Add ¼ cup (35g) dried cranberries, 1 star anise, 1 tablespoon harissa paste, 1 teaspoon freshly ground black pepper, 1 teaspoon fine salt, 1⅔ cups (410ml) red wine vinegar and 1⅓ cups (295g) brown sugar; stir to combine. Bring to a simmer over medium heat, stirring until sugar dissolves. Reduce heat to low. Simmer for 20 minutes or until plums are tender. Coarsely chop 1 bunch (500g) rhubarb and add to saucepan. Cook, stirring occasionally, for 25 minutes or until chutney is thick and jammy. Transfer to a sterilised jar (see page 160). Store in the fridge for up to 1 month.

TIP *Use the ratio 3:4 sugar to vinegar to make chutneys using other fruits and vegetables.*

PREP + COOK TIME 1 HOUR **MAKES** 12

BAKED BHAJIS WITH GREEN CHUTNEY

THESE BITES ARE ALSO AIR FRYER FRIENDLY; PLACE BHAJIS IN A 180°C PREHEATED AIRFRYER FOR 10 MINUTES OR UNTIL CRISP AND GOLDEN BROWN.

2 tsp coriander seeds
2 tbsp cumin seeds
2 large onions (400g), sliced (see swap ins)
1 small leek (200g), sliced (see swap ins)
1 tsp fine salt
2 tbsp neutral oil (see tips)
2 tsp ground turmeric
⅔ cup (100g) chickpea flour (besan) (see swap ins)
2 tbsp rice flour
1 tsp bicarbonate of soda
1 egg white (see waste not)
cooking oil spray (see tips)
2 tbsp sea salt flakes
plain yoghurt, small red chillies, coriander leaves and lime wedges, to serve

GREEN CHUTNEY

2 bunches coriander, stems and roots
1 tbsp lime pickle (see swap ins)
1 tbsp grated ginger

1 Preheat oven to 180°C/160°C fan-forced.

2 Place coriander and cumin seeds in a frying pan; toast over medium-high heat for 2 minutes or until fragrant. Reserve half the toasted seeds in a bowl and crush remaining seeds into a fine powder using a mortar and pestle (see tips).

3 Place onion, leek, fine salt and crushed seeds in a large bowl. Using your hands, scrunch and rub the mixture together until well combined. Set aside for 10 minutes.

4 Meanwhile, make the green chutney: Blend or process ingredients with ¼ cup (60ml) water until smooth. Season to taste.

5 Add oil, turmeric, flours, bicarb and egg white to the onion-leek mixture; mix until well combined.

6 Drop ⅓-cup scoops of the bhaji batter onto a lined oven tray; spray with oil. Bake for 35 minutes until golden brown.

7 Meanwhile, add salt flakes to reserved toasted seeds in bowl; rub to combine.

8 Serve bhajis with yoghurt, green chutney, chillies, coriander leaves, spiced salt and lime wedges.

TIPS *Neutral oils include vegetable, sunflower, grapeseed, peanut and rice bran. If you don't have oil spray, you could lightly brush the bhajis with extra oil. If you don't have a mortar and pestle, you could process the spices in a small food processor.*

SWAP INS *Instead of onions and leeks, use whichever alliums you have on hand. To keep this gluten free, swap chickpea flour for almond, quinoa or cassava flour, or alternatively use plain flour. Instead of lime pickle, you could use the finely grated rind and juice of 1 lime or lemon.*

WASTE NOT

SAVE THE LEFTOVER EGG YOLK TO MAKE THE SESAME CHEESE BISCUITS, PAGE 65.

TIPS

YOU COULD USE A VARIETY OF ALLIUMS, SUCH AS RED AND BROWN ONION, LEEK, AND SHALLOTS. IF USING GARLIC, ROAST IN THE SKIN, THEN PRESS TO REMOVE THE FLESH.

PREP + COOK TIME 45 MINUTES **SERVES** 6

CHARRED ONION POTATO SALAD

SPROUTING ONIONS AND GARLIC ARE STILL SAFE TO EAT. GIVE THEM A SECOND LIFE BY LIGHTLY CHARRING THEM IN THE OVEN FOR A BITTER-SWEET FLAVOUR, AS WE'VE DONE HERE.

1.5kg potatoes, skin on
800g alliums of your choice, chopped coarsely (see tips)
2 tbsp olive oil

DRESSING
⅔ cup (200g) mayonnaise
½ cup (120g) sour cream
⅔ cup (120g) finely chopped gherkins (see swap ins)
1 tbsp gherkin brine
2 tsp Dijon mustard (see swap ins)
1 lemon, rind finely grated, then juiced
¼ cup (60ml) olive oil
½ cup parsley, stems and leaves, chopped coarsely, plus extra leaves to serve (see swap ins)

1 Preheat oven to 200°C/180°C fan-forced.

2 Halve any large potatoes. Cook potatoes in a saucepan of salted boiling water for 20 minutes or until tender. Drain then set aside to cool.

3 Meanwhile, place alliums on a lined oven tray; drizzle with oil and season. Roast for 20 minutes or until tender and slightly charred.

4 Make the dressing: Whisk ingredients in a large bowl until well combined. Season to taste.

5 Add potatoes and two-thirds of the charred alliums to the dressing in the bowl; toss to combine and season to taste.

6 Serve potato salad topped with remaining charred alliums and extra parsley leaves; season with freshly ground pepper.

SWAP INS *Instead of gherkins, you could use capers, olives or any other pickled vegetable. Use wholegrain mustard instead of Dijon mustard. Swap parsley, with dill, chives, mint or basil.*

LEFTOVERS
LEFTOVERS
LEFTOVERS
LEFTOVERS
LEFTOVERS
LEFTOVERS

PREP + COOK TIME 25 MINUTES **MAKES** 4

PASTA & GARLIC BREAD TOASTIES

IF YOU DON'T HAVE A SANDWICH PRESS, COOK THE SANDWICHES IN A FRYING PAN OVER MEDIUM-HIGH HEAT, PRESSING DOWN WITH A SPATULA FOR AN EVEN GOLDEN COLOUR.

2 large tomatoes (500g), chopped coarsely
1½ tsp caster sugar
1 tbsp olive oil
125g butter, softened
4 cloves garlic, crushed
1 tbsp finely chopped parsley
8 slices white bread
1½ cups (220g) leftover cooked pasta
2 cups (200g) grated cheese (see swap ins)

1 Blend or process tomato, sugar and oil; transfer to a medium saucepan. Cook sauce over low heat, stirring occasionally, for 10 minutes or until slightly reduced; season to taste.

2 Meanwhile, combine butter, garlic and parsley in a small bowl; season to taste. Spread garlic butter over one side of each bread slice.

3 Add pasta and cheese to tomato sauce; stir to combine. Divide pasta mixture among the unbuttered side of 4 bread slices. Sandwich together with remaining bread slices, buttered-side up.

4 In batches, cook sandwiches in a sandwich press or jaffle machine for 4 minutes or until golden and cheese is melted (see note above).

SWAP INS *You could use a mixture of melting cheeses, such as cheddar, Gruyère, haloumi, havarti, parmesan and gouda.*

CHEESY

SWAP INS

INSTEAD OF SPAGHETTI, YOU COULD USE ANY COOKED PASTA SHAPE YOU HAVE ON HAND. USE THE PESTO ON PAGE 96, OR ENJOY WITH YOUR FAVOURITE CONDIMENT.

PREP + COOK TIME 25 MINUTES **MAKES** 8

CACIO E PEPE FRITTERS

TOSS LEFTOVER COOKED PASTA IN OIL BEFORE STORING TO PREVENT THE STRANDS FROM STICKING TOGETHER.

20g butter
¼ cup (35g) plain flour
¾ cup (180ml) milk, warmed
1 cup (80g) finely grated parmesan, plus extra shaved to serve
1 tsp freshly ground black pepper
2 cups (300g) leftover cooked spaghetti (see swap ins)
⅓ cup (80ml) olive oil
pesto (see swap ins) and basil leaves, to serve

1 Place butter in a small saucepan and melt over medium heat. Add flour and stir for 1 minute or until sandy. Gradually add milk, whisking continuously, until smooth and combined. Add parmesan and pepper; whisk for 1 minute or until melted and slightly thickened. Season to taste.

2 Add pasta to cheese sauce and mix until well combined. Divide pasta mixture into eight round portions; place on a lined tray.

3 Heat oil in a large frying pan over medium-high heat. Cook fritters for 2 minutes each side or until golden. Transfer to a wire rack.

4 Serve fritters warm, topped with pesto, basil leaves and extra shaved parmesan; season with freshly ground pepper.

PREP + COOK TIME 35 MINUTES **SERVES** 4

SMOKY HAM BAKED BEANS

USE WHICHEVER LEGUMES YOU HAVE ON HAND; WE'VE USED A MIX OF CANNELLINI AND BUTTER BEANS. YOU COULD ALSO COOK 300G DRIED LEGUMES OR USE 2 X 400G CANS OF DRAINED BEANS.

2 tbsp olive oil
1 medium onion (150g), chopped finely
1 medium capsicum (200g), sliced thinly
4 cloves garlic, crushed
2 tbsp rosemary leaves, chopped (see swap ins)
1 tbsp smoked paprika
1 cup (250ml) stock (chicken or vegetable) or water
500g smoked ham hock, chopped (see swap ins)
700g tomato passata
2 tbsp brown sugar
500g leftover cooked legumes (see note above)
finely grated parmesan, sliced chives and chargrilled bread, to serve

1 Heat oil in a large saucepan over medium heat. Cook onion and capsicum for 4 minutes or until starting to soften.

2 Add garlic and rosemary; cook for 4 minutes or until capsicum is tender. Add paprika and stir for 30 seconds or until fragrant.

3 Add stock, ham hock, passata and sugar; bring to the boil. Reduce heat to medium. Simmer for 10 minutes or until thickened slightly. Stir in legumes; season to taste.

4 Top beans with grated parmesan and chives; season with freshly ground pepper. Serve with chargrilled bread.

SWAP INS *Instead of rosemary, you could also use thyme, sage or oregano. Swap the smoked ham hock with bacon, chorizo, pancetta or pork sausages.*

SAUCY

SWAP INS

✱ ✱ ✱

YOU CAN USE A COMBINATION OF SOFT HERBS, INCLUDING MINT, CORIANDER, BASIL, PARSLEY, DILL OR CHIVES. INCLUDE BOTH THE STEMS AND LEAVES.

PREP + COOK TIME 40 MINUTES (+ FREEZING) **SERVES** 4

GREEN FALAFELS WITH TAHINI YOGHURT

WE USED CHICKPEAS, BUT USE WHICHEVER LEGUMES YOU HAVE ON HAND. YOU COULD ALSO COOK 150G DRIED SOAKED BEANS OR USE A 400G CAN OF DRAINED BEANS.

2 cups (300g) peas, thawed
2 cups (250g) leftover cooked legumes (see note above)
1 medium onion (150g), chopped coarsely
3 cloves garlic, plus 1 clove extra, crushed
2½ cups coarsely chopped soft herbs (see swap ins), plus extra to serve
⅓ cup (50g) plain flour
1 tsp fine salt
2 tsp ground cumin
2 shallots (50g), sliced thinly
2½ tbsp lemon juice
½ cup (140g) Greek yoghurt
1½ tbsp tahini
neutral oil, for deep-frying (see tip)
charred pitta or flatbreads, lemon wedges, za'atar (optional) and olive oil, to serve

1 Blend or process peas, legumes, onion, garlic, herbs, flour, salt and cumin until finely chopped; season. Shape 2 heaped tablespoons of mixture into rounds and place on a lined tray. Freeze for 20 minutes or until firm.

2 Meanwhile, combine shallots and 2 tablespoons of the lemon juice in a small bowl; set aside to pickle. Drain before serving.

3 Place yoghurt, tahini, extra crushed garlic and remaining lemon juice in a bowl; whisk until smooth. Season to taste.

4 Fill a large saucepan one-third full with oil; heat to 180°C (or until the oil sizzles when a small cube of bread is added). In batches, fry falafel, turning occasionally, for 4 minutes or until golden all over. Remove with a slotted spoon; drain on paper towel.

5 Serve falafel with extra soft herbs, tahini yoghurt, pickled shallot, charred pitta and lemon wedges; sprinkle with za'atar and drizzle with olive oil.

TIP *Use any neutral oil, including vegetable, sunflower, grapeseed, peanut and rice bran.*

CRISPY
CRUNCHY

VEGIE PIES

USE FILLO OR PUFF PASTRY TO EFFORTLESSLY TURN LEFTOVERS INTO PIES FOR A SECOND MEAL. BE AS CREATIVE AS YOU LIKE – USE THESE RECIPES AS A FOUNDATION FOR A VARIETY OF TOPPINGS AND FILLINGS (SEE SWAP INS).

ROAST VEGIE SLICE

PREP + COOK TIME 25 MINUTES
SERVES 2

Preheat oven to 200°C/180°C fan-forced. Cut 1 sheet thawed puff pastry in half and place on a lined oven tray. Score a 1cm edge inside each rectangle; spread 1 tablespoon salsa verde (see page 96; see swap ins) inside each border. Thinly slice leftover roast pumpkin (see swap ins) and divide between pastry halves; season to taste. Bake for 15 minutes or until golden brown. Top with crumbled goat's cheese (see swap ins) and red veined sorrel, if you like.

SWAP INS *Instead of salsa verde, you could spread the base with any thick mild sauce, such as harissa or pesto. Use any leftover roast vegies you have on hand. Instead of goat's cheese, top with your favourite cheese.*

FILLO CURRY PIE

PREP + COOK TIME 35 MINUTES
SERVES 4

Preheat oven to 200°C/180°C fan-forced. Grease a 20cm (8 cup) baking dish. Add 6 cups (800g) leftover curry (see swap ins) and 2 cups (300g) mixed vegetables (see swap ins) to dish; stir to combine. Season to taste. Place 4 sheets fillo pastry and 2 tablespoons olive oil in a medium bowl; using your hands, scrunch fillo until well coated in the oil. Arrange fillo on top of the curry mixture. Bake for 25 minutes or until golden brown. Top with fried curry leaves, if you like.

SWAP INS *Instead of curry, you could use other saucy leftovers, such as a stew, ragù or tagine. Use any vegetables you have on hand, such as frozen peas, coarsely chopped carrots, green beans or capsicums.*

PREP + COOK TIME 45 MINUTES **SERVES** 4

LEBANESE LENTIL RICE BOWLS

BAHARAT HAS A SWEET AND SMOKY FLAVOUR, BUT YOU COULD ALSO USE A COMBINATION OF SMOKED PAPRIKA, CUMIN, CINNAMON AND PEPPER. WE'VE USED BASMATI, BUT ANY COOKED RICE WILL BE DELICIOUS.

¼ red cabbage (350g), sliced thinly (see waste not)
2 tbsp lemon juice (see swap ins)
4 cloves garlic, crushed
1 small bunch each parsley, mint and dill (see swap ins)
½ tsp sumac, plus extra to serve
½ cup (125ml) olive oil
1 large pitta bread, cut into small pieces (see swap ins)
2 large red onions (400g), sliced thinly
2 tsp Baharat (see note above)
4 cups (600g) leftover cooked rice (see note above)
400g can lentils, drained, rinsed
2 tsp finely grated lemon rind
1 cup (280g) Greek yoghurt

1 Preheat oven to 180°C/160°C fan-forced.

2 Place cabbage, lemon juice and a quarter of the garlic in a large bowl and season generously; toss to combine.

3 Pick herb leaves and finely chop the stems.

4 Combine sumac and 2 tablespoons of the oil in a medium bowl; season. Add pitta and toss to coat. Spread pitta over a lined oven tray. Bake for 5 minutes or until golden and crisp.

5 Meanwhile, heat remaining oil in a large frying pan over high heat. Cook three-quarters of the onion, stirring continuously, for 6 minutes or until golden. Using a slotted spoon, transfer to paper towel.

6 Reduce heat to medium-high. In same pan, cook remaining onion, stirring, for 3 minutes or until lightly golden. Add remaining garlic, the Baharat and herb stems; cook for 1 minute. Add rice and lentils; cook, stirring, for 6 minutes or until heated through. Stir in lemon rind and season to taste.

7 Add herb leaves to cabbage salad and toss to combine.

8 Spread yoghurt over the base of serving bowls; top with lentil rice, cabbage salad, fried onions and toasted pitta. Dust with extra sumac.

SWAP INS *Instead of lemon, you could use another citrus or vinegar. Mix and swap fresh herbs to suit whichever you have on hand. Swap pitta bread with sourdough bread, tortillas or wraps.*

WASTE NOT

* * *

RESERVE ANY REMAINING CABBAGE TO MAKE THE CHARRED CABBAGE WITH BLUE CHEESE DRESSING, PAGE 32, OR THE TOMATO & CABBAGE TABBOULEH, PAGE 35.

TIP

IF YOU DON'T HAVE A MORTAR AND PESTLE, YOU COULD CRUSH THE SEEDS AND NUTS IN A SMALL FOOD PROCESSOR OR BY USING THE END OF A ROLLING PIN.

PREP + COOK TIME 40 MINUTES **MAKES** 12

PEANUT ONIGIRI

PICK YOUR FAVOURITE JAPANESE CONDIMENTS TO SERVE ALONGSIDE THESE RICE BALLS. INSTEAD OF FRYING, YOU COULD ALSO SERVE THE ONIGIRI FRESH, WHICH IS EQUALLY DELICIOUS.

---

2 tbsp rice wine vinegar
2 tbsp caster sugar
1 tsp fine salt
4 cups (600g) leftover cooked shortgrain rice, heated
2 nori (seaweed) sheets, cut into 12 strips
sesame oil, for drizzling
soy sauce, for brushing, plus extra to serve
shichimi togarashi, wasabi, pickled ginger and avocado slices, to serve

PEANUT FILLING

2 tbsp sesame seeds
2 tbsp salted peanuts
1 tbsp sesame oil
4 green onions, sliced thinly

1 Make the peanut filling: Toast sesame seeds in a small frying pan over medium heat for 5 minutes or until golden. Lightly crush toasted seeds and peanuts using a mortar and pestle (see tip). Heat sesame oil in same frying pan over medium-high heat. Cook green onion for 1 minute or until bright green; transfer to peanut mixture and stir to combine. Season to taste.

2 Combine vinegar, sugar and salt in a large bowl; stir until sugar dissolves. Add rice and stir to coat. Blend or process half the rice mixture until sticky; return to bowl and stir to combine.

3 Using damp hands, divide the rice mixture into 12 round portions. Working with one at a time, use your finger to make an indent in the middle of each rice ball; fill with 2 teaspoons of the peanut filling. Shape rice around the filling to enclose, then press into a triangular shape. Place a nori strip over the base and fold up to the middle of each side. Repeat with remaining rice, filling and nori strips.

4 Drizzle each side of the onigiri with sesame oil. Heat a large frying pan over medium heat. Cook onigiri, turning regularly, for 6 minutes or until golden and crisp. In the last minute, brush each side with soy sauce.

5 Sprinkle onigiri with shichimi togarashi. Serve warm with extra soy sauce, wasabi, pickled ginger and avocado.

PREP + COOK TIME 45 MINUTES **SERVES** 2

CORN CHIP CHILLI TRAYBAKE

YOU COULD ALSO SERVE THE CHILLI WITH RICE AND A DOLLOP OF SOUR CREAM OR YOGHURT.

1 tbsp olive oil
1 small red onion (100g), chopped finely
1 medium red or green capsicum (200g), chopped finely
1 tbsp Mexican spice mix (see swap ins)
400g can black beans, drained, rinsed
3 cups (300g) leftover Bolognese
2 cobs corn in husks (800g)
200g corn chips
¼ cup (50g) fetta, crumbled
1 long chilli, sliced thinly
coriander leaves (see swap ins), lime wedges (see swap ins) and hot sauce, to serve

GUACAMOLE

1 medium avocado (250g)
1 small clove garlic, crushed
1 tbsp lime juice
½ cup coriander, stems and leaves, chopped finely

1 Heat oil in a saucepan over medium heat. Cook onion and capsicum for 5 minutes or until onion softens.

2 Add spice mix; cook, stirring, for 1 minute. Stir in black beans, Bolognese and ½ cup (125ml) water; bring to the boil. Reduce heat to low. Cook for 15 minutes or until reduced. Season to taste.

3 Meanwhile, cook corn cobs in a large saucepan of boiling salted water for 6 minutes or until almost tender. Drain and cool.

4 Preheat a grill plate or barbecue. Peel back the corn husks; remove and discard the silks. Cook corn on grill plate or barbecue for 5 minutes or until tender and grill marks appear. Transfer to a plate. Cut the kernels from the cobs in sections if possible.

5 Preheat oven grill to high. Arrange corn chips on an oven tray; top with Bolognese chilli, corn kernels and fetta. Grill for 5 minutes or until corn chips are lightly charred.

6 Meanwhile, make the guacamole: Mash ingredients together in a bowl until well combined. Season to taste.

7 Top corn chip chilli with guacamole, sliced chilli and coriander leaves; season with freshly ground pepper. Serve with lime wedges and hot sauce.

TIPS *If you have extra vegies such as celery or carrot, chop finely and cook with the onion in step 1.*

SWAP INS *Instead of the Mexican spice mix, you could use a combination of cumin, chilli flakes, dried oregano and paprika. Swap coriander with mint or parsley. Instead of lime, you could use lemon.*

CRISPY
CRUNCHY

PREP + COOK TIME 15 MINUTES **SERVES** 4

SLOPPY JOES

MAKE THESE ROLLS YOUR OWN AND FILL WITH A VARIETY OF YOUR FAVOURITE ACCOMPANIMENTS, SUCH AS PICKLED JALAPEÑO, CARAMELISED ONION OR EVEN A FRIED EGG.

3 cups (300g) leftover Bolognese
2 tbsp smoky barbecue sauce
1 tbsp Worcestershire sauce
1 tbsp vinegar (see swap ins)
4 bread rolls (400g), halved
1 baby cos lettuce (180g), leaves separated (see swap ins)
1 cup (120g) baby cornichons, sliced thinly, plus extra whole to serve
⅓ cup (40g) grated cheddar
potato chips, to serve

1 Place Bolognese, sauces and vinegar in a small saucepan; heat over medium heat until bubbling. Season to taste.

2 Place bread rolls, cut-side down, in a large frying pan over medium-high; toast for 3 minutes or until golden (see tip).

3 Divide lettuce between bread roll bases; top each with ¾ cup of Bolognese mixture, cornichons and cheddar, then roll tops. Serve with potato chips and extra cornichons.

TIP *You could also toast the bread rolls under the grill or in a toaster.*

SWAP INS *We used apple cider vinegar, but use whichever vinegar you have on hand. Instead of cos lettuce, you could use other fresh leafy greens, such as baby spinach or rocket, or a slaw mix.*

PREP + COOK TIME 40 MINUTES **MAKES** 15

PANTRY COMPOST COOKIES

TRANSFORM USED COFFEE GROUNDS AND ACCUMULATED PANTRY ITEMS INTO THESE SALTY-SWEET COOKIES. USE THE MEASUREMENTS AS A GUIDE AND BUILD YOUR DOUGH USING WHICHEVER INGREDIENTS YOU HAVE ON HAND.

---

1 cup (150g) plain flour
½ tsp bicarbonate of soda
½ tsp baking powder
¼ tsp fine salt
110g butter, softened
½ cup (110g) caster sugar
½ cup (110g) brown sugar
1½ tbsp leftover coffee grounds (see tips)
1 egg
1 tbsp milk (see swap ins)
½ cup (90g) rolled oats
½ cup (40g) shredded coconut
½ cup (80g) mixed roasted nuts, chopped
125g dark chocolate, chopped
1 tbsp sea salt flakes

TOPPING

1 tbsp rolled oats
1 tbsp shredded coconut
2 tbsp mixed roasted nuts
2 tbsp coarsely chopped dark chocolate

1 Preheat oven to 180°C/160°C fan-forced. Line three large oven trays with baking paper.

2 Combine flour, bicarb, baking powder and salt in a large bowl.

3 Make the topping: Combine ingredients in a medium bowl.

4 Place butter, sugars and coffee grounds in a large bowl; using an electric mixer, beat for 8 minutes or until light and fluffy. Add egg and beat until well combined. Add milk and beat until combined.

5 Add the flour mixture to coffee mixture; beat on low speed until just combined. Fold in oats, coconut, nuts and chocolate.

6 Roll 2 tablespoons of dough into balls (see tips) and place 5cm apart on lined oven trays. Using lightly oiled hands, press dough balls down until about 5mm thick.

7 Bake cookies for 10 minutes. Remove from the oven and sprinkle topping mixture and salt flakes over each cookie. Return to the oven. Bake for a further 5–8 minutes or until cookies are golden. Set aside to cool on trays.

TIPS *Store used ground coffee in an airtight container in the fridge until required. You could also use a quick-release ice-cream scoop to portion the cookie dough.*

SWAP INS

WE USED FULL CREAM MILK, BUT USE WHICHEVER MILK IS YOUR PREFERENCE.

WASTE NOT

✱ ✱ ✱

RESERVE ANY REMAINING CABBAGE TO MAKE THE CHARRED CABBAGE WITH BLUE CHEESE DRESSING, PAGE 32, OR THE TOMATO & CABBAGE TABBOULEH, PAGE 35.

PREP + COOK TIME 50 MINUTES (+ STANDING) **SERVES** 4

SPICED COFFEE-RUBBED STEAK WITH SLAW

DON'T WORRY IF YOU DON'T HAVE ALL THE SPICES; USE WHATEVER YOU HAVE AVAILABLE, OR SWAP FOR A STORE-BOUGHT SMOKY AMERICAN SPICE BLEND.

4 x 200g sirloin steaks
2 corn cobs (800g), husks and silks removed
⅓ cup (80ml) olive oil
¼ green cabbage (400g), shredded (see waste not)
2 small baby cos lettuce (360g), torn (see swap ins)
2 green onions (20g), sliced thinly
2 jalapeños, chopped finely
1 bunch coriander, stems chopped finely, leaves picked (see swap ins)

SPICED COFFEE RUB

2 tbsp leftover coffee grounds
1 tbsp smoked paprika
2 tsp ground cumin
2 tsp ground coriander
2 tsp onion powder
2 tsp garlic powder
1½ tsp salt flakes
1 tsp ground chipotle
1 tsp chilli flakes
½ tsp freshly ground pepper

YOGHURT DRESSING

¼ cup (60ml) milk
2 tbsp Greek yoghurt
2 limes, rind finely grated, then juiced, plus extra wedges to serve
2 tbsp olive oil
2 tbsp mayonnaise
1 clove garlic, crushed

1 Make the spiced coffee rub: Combine ingredients in a medium bowl. (Makes ½ cup.)

2 Pat steaks dry with paper towel. Place ⅓ cup spiced coffee rub (see waste not) and steaks in a large bowl; thoroughly rub spiced coffee rub over steaks. Set aside for 30 minutes.

3 Meanwhile, make the yoghurt dressing: Whisk ingredients in a bowl until well combined. Season to taste.

4 Preheat a grill plate or barbecue. Toss corn and 1 tablespoon of the oil in a medium bowl until well coated; season to taste. Cook corn on heated grill plate or barbecue, turning, for 10 minutes or until tender and lightly charred. Transfer to a plate. Cut the kernels from the cobs in sections if possible.

5 Drizzle remaining oil over steaks. Cook steaks on heated grill plate or barbecue, turning every minute, for 6–8 minutes for medium-rare, or until cooked to your liking. Transfer to a plate; rest for 5 minutes.

6 Combine cabbage, lettuce, green onion, chopped jalapeño, coriander, charred corn and half the dressing in a large bowl; season to taste.

7 Thickly slice the steak and serve with slaw and extra lime wedges. Drizzle remaining dressing over the slaw.

SWAP INS *Instead of baby cos, you could use whichever leafy greens you have on hand. Instead of coriander, you could use mint, parsley, dill or chives.*

NO WASTE *Store remaining coffee rub in the fridge for up to 1 week. Use to flavour or marinate other proteins.*

YOUR POSITIVE IMPACT

* * *

We all have the power to positively impact the environment through our daily food habits. It's not so much about what you eat but how what you eat was grown, how it got to you and what you do with it. The way we choose to eat can regenerate the world.

If we can start to 'close the loop' in our kitchens, there is so much potential for change.

Your daily food choices can support the production of food within your local community and create better food security. Having reliable access to a sufficient quantity of affordable and nutritious non-toxic food should be a number one priority for us all. Your choices around food can restore our soil and turn climate change around.

HERE ARE SOME QUESTIONS TO CONSIDER WHEN YOU'RE PURCHASING FOOD

Where does it come from?

What is the hidden environmental or social cost?

Was it grown regeneratively or conventionally using chemicals?

Where was it grown?

Was it transported a long distance?

What and who am I supporting by buying this?

Is it whole food or highly processed?

How is it packaged?

Can the packaging be reused, composted or recycled?

Will any of it be wasted?

FOOD WASTE FACTS

When it comes to food, Australia and New Zealand are big consumers and some of the most wasteful nations in the world.

Australians throw out 7.3 million tonnes of food every year. New Zealanders throw out about 157,389 tonnes. Most of this is still perfectly edible.

When food waste ends up in landfill (instead of compost), it rots and releases methane gas. This is one of the main gases contributing to climate change, and it's 28 times more potent than carbon dioxide.

When food scraps turn into compost, more carbon is stored in the soil, helping to reduce the effects of climate change.

The top five most wasted foods in Australia are vegetables, bread, fruit, bagged salad and leftovers.

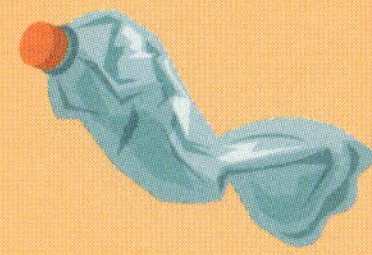

47% of all plastic waste comes from our homes. Recycling rates are less than 60% (on average across Australia and New Zealand).

PREP + COOK TIME 50 MINUTES **MAKES** 8

ALOO CHICKEN PATTIES

THIS CRUMBED AND FRIED PAKISTANI SNACK CAN BE FROZEN AFTER STEP 3; WHEN READY TO SERVE, JUST DEFROST AND FRY. ENJOY AS IS OR USE TO FILL SANDWICHES OR BURGERS.

2 cups (500g) leftover mashed potato
500g cooked chicken, shredded (see tips)
2 tsp fine salt
1½ tsp freshly ground black pepper
½ tsp garam masala
1 tsp ground coriander
2 cloves garlic, crushed
1 tsp ginger, chopped finely
2 long red or green chillies, seeded, chopped finely
½ cup coriander, chopped coarsely, plus extra to serve
2 eggs, beaten lightly
1 cup (100g) fine breadcrumbs
½ cup (125ml) neutral oil (see tips)
¼ cup (70g) tamarind chutney (see swap ins)
¾ cup (240g) Greek yoghurt
lime wedges, to serve

1 Place mashed potato, chicken, salt, pepper, garam masala, ground coriander, garlic, ginger, chilli and coriander in a large bowl; mix well to combine. Season to taste.

2 Shape ½-cup portions of chicken-mash mixture into patties, about 2cm thick, and place on a lined tray.

3 Place egg and breadcrumbs in separate medium bowls. In batches, dip patties in egg, then press in breadcrumbs to coat; place on a plate. Repeat with remaining patties.

4 Heat oil in a large, deep frying pan over medium-high heat. Fry patties for 2 minutes each side or until golden brown and heated through. Drain on paper towel. Season with salt.

5 Combine tamarind chutney and yoghurt in a small bowl; season to taste.

6 Serve patties warm with yoghurt sauce, lime wedges and extra coriander.

SWAP INS *Instead of tamarind chutney, you could use whichever chutney you have on hand, or omit it and serve with just the yoghurt.*

TIPS *If you don't have cooked chicken, poach 700g chicken thighs in 2 cups (500ml) chicken stock in a medium saucepan for 30 minutes or until cooked through. Drain then cool and finely shred. Neutral oils include vegetable, sunflower, grapeseed, peanut and rice bran.*

TASTY

SWAP INS

INSTEAD OF CORIANDER, YOU COULD USE CHIVES, MINT OR PARSLEY.

PREP + COOK TIME 25 MINUTES **SERVES** 6 (AS A SNACK)

LOADED POTATO SKINS

RESERVE ANY POTATO SKINS TO CREATE THESE CRISPY STUFFED BITES. ALTERNATIVELY, YOU COULD BAKE YOUR POTATO PEELINGS INTO CHIPS AND SERVE WITH THE BELOW FILLINGS.

8 large leftover potato skins (500g) (see tip)
olive oil cooking spray
1 cup (120g) hard cheese, grated
1 small red onion (80g), sliced thinly
1 large tomato (220g), seeded, chopped finely
2 tbsp finely chopped coriander, plus extra leaves to serve (see swap ins)
1 clove garlic, crushed
2 tbsp lime juice
1 tbsp olive oil
1 large avocado (320g), mashed
lime wedges, to serve

1 Preheat oven to 220°C/200°C fan-forced.

2 Spray potato skins with oil and season to taste.

3 Bake potato skins for 5 minutes. Scatter with cheese, then return to the oven. Bake for a further 5 minutes or until golden and crisp.

4 Meanwhile, combine onion, tomato, coriander, garlic, lime juice and oil in a medium bowl; season to taste.

5 Fill crisp potato skins with tomato salsa and top with avocado and extra coriander leaves; season with freshly ground pepper. Serve with lime wedges.

TIP *If you don't have potato skins, preheat oven to 220°C/200°C fan-forced. Scrub 1kg potatoes and prick each with a fork; place on a lined oven tray. Bake for 1 hour or until tender. Halve potatoes lengthways and scoop out the flesh. Continue recipe from step 1. Reserve potato flesh for Aloo Chicken Patties, page 136, if you like.*

SERVING SUGGESTIONS
Serve with your favourite taco-inspired fillings, such as sour cream, black beans, charred corn or even leftover taco mince.

PREP + COOK TIME 55 MINUTES (+ COOLING) **SERVES** 6–8

4-INGREDIENT ICE-CREAM CAKE

IF YOU DON'T HAVE FROZEN BERRIES, USE WHICHEVER FRUIT YOU HAVE ON HAND. WE USED VANILLA ICE-CREAM, BUT USE YOUR FLAVOUR OF CHOICE.

300g frozen mixed berries
3 cups (750ml) leftover ice-cream, melted
1½ cups (225g) self-raising flour
2½ cups (400g) icing sugar

1 Place berries in a sieve over a medium bowl. Set aside to thaw. Reserve the drained berry juice; you will need 3 tablespoons (see tip).

2 Preheat oven to 200°C/180°C fan-forced. Grease and line a 1-litre (4-cup) loaf pan.

3 Place ice-cream, flour and a pinch of salt in a large bowl; fold together until just combined. Add the thawed berries; fold until just combined.

4 Pour the batter into the loaf pan; gently tap the pan on the bench to remove any air pockets. Bake for 45 minutes or until a skewer inserted in the centre comes out clean. Cool in the pan for 10 minutes. Turn out onto a serving plate and cool completely.

5 Add icing sugar to reserved berry juice and mix until well combined.

6 Drizzle berry icing over cake.

TIP *If you don't have enough berry juice, add enough citrus juice to make up the liquid quantity.*

SWAP INS

WE USED VANILLA ICE-CREAM, BUT USE WHICHEVER FLAVOUR YOU HAVE ON HAND.

PREP + COOK TIME 20 MINUTES **SERVES** 4

CINNAMON & COCONUT FRENCH TOAST

ANOTHER PERFECT USE FOR STALE BREAD! WE PREFER A CHEWY LOAF, SUCH AS SOURDOUGH, ALTHOUGH ANY BREAD WILL BE DELICIOUS.

1 tbsp caster sugar
½ tsp ground cinnamon
1 cup (75g) shredded coconut, toasted
½ tsp salt flakes
3 cups (750ml) leftover ice-cream, melted (see swap ins)
butter, for frying
8 thick slices bread (see note above)
chopped strawberries and maple syrup, to serve

1 Combine sugar, cinnamon, coconut and salt in a wide, shallow bowl. Place ice-cream in a second wide, shallow bowl.

2 Melt butter in a large frying pan over medium heat. Working in batches, turn and press bread in ice-cream until well coated. Cook for 2 minutes each side or until golden. Press French toast on both sides in coconut mixture to coat. Transfer to a plate and cover to keep warm. Repeat with remaining bread, melting more butter in pan as needed.

3 Serve French toast warm, topped with any remaining coconut mixture and the chopped strawberries; drizzle with maple syrup.

PREP + COOK TIME 20 MINUTES (+ STANDING) **SERVES** 2

GREEK FETTA WRAPS

TOSSING LEFTOVER MEAT IN THE GARLIC-OREGANO INFUSED FETTA WILL GIVE PRE-COOKED CUTS A NEW LEASE OF LIFE. USE EITHER LAMB, PORK OR BEEF.

1 small red onion (100g), sliced thinly
⅓ cup (80ml) red wine vinegar (see swap ins)
1 tbsp caster sugar
⅓ cup (80ml) olive oil
1 tbsp oregano, chopped finely (see swap ins)
3 cloves garlic, crushed
100g fetta, crumbled
250g leftover roast meat, chopped (see note above)
1 fennel bulb (300g), sliced thinly, fronds reserved (see swap ins)
½ cup (80g) mixed olives
2 large pitta breads, grilled
½ cup (140g) Greek yoghurt

1 Combine onion, ¼ cup (60ml) of the vinegar and the sugar in a small bowl. Set aside for 20 minutes. Drain before serving.

2 Meanwhile, heat ¼ cup (60ml) of the oil, the oregano and garlic in a small frying pan over medium heat; stir for 2 minutes or until fragrant. Transfer to a medium bowl. Add fetta and toss to combine.

3 Add roast meat to fetta mixture and toss to coat. Season to taste.

4 Combine fennel and olives with remaining oil and vinegar in a bowl; season to taste.

5 Spread grilled pitta breads with yoghurt; top with fennel salad, meat and fetta mixture, pickled onions and reserved fennel fronds.

SWAP INS *Instead of red wine vinegar, you could use whichever vinegar you have on hand. Swap oregano with rosemary or dried oregano. Instead of fennel, you could use leafy greens, celery, radishes or cucumber.*

TASTY

PREP + COOK TIME 1 HOUR 10 MINUTES SERVES 4

RED WINE STEW WITH PARMESAN DUMPLINGS

LARGE CUTS OF MEAT, SUCH AS LAMB SHOULDER OR PORK BELLY, WORK BEST FOR THIS RECIPE.

2 tbsp olive oil
350g pancetta, chopped (see swap ins)
1 large red onion (300g), cut into thick wedges
2 cloves garlic, crushed
1 medium carrot (120g), chopped
2 trimmed celery stalks (200g), sliced thickly
1 cup (250ml) dry red wine
400g can diced tomatoes
2 bay leaves
500g leftover roast meat, chopped (see note above)
1 cup (150g) plain flour
1 cup (150g) self-raising flour
125g chilled butter, grated
½ cup (40g) finely grated parmesan, plus extra to serve (see swap ins)

1 Heat oil in a Dutch oven or flameproof casserole dish over medium heat. Cook pancetta and onion, stirring, for 2 minutes or until pancetta is golden. Add garlic, carrot and celery; cook for 5 minutes or until slightly softened. Add wine, tomatoes and bay leaves; bring to a simmer. Cook, stirring occasionally, for 10 minutes or until reduced. Stir through roast meat; season to taste.

2 Meanwhile, preheat oven to 180°C/160°C fan-forced.

3 Process flours, butter and ½ cup (125ml) chilled water until the dough just comes together. Turn dough out onto a lightly floured surface and press into a 1cm thick round. Using a 6.5cm round cutter, cut rounds from dough. Press remaining dough together and repeat cutting to make 12 dumplings in total.

4 Arrange dumplings on stew; sprinkle over parmesan. Bake for 30 minutes or until dumplings are cooked through and golden brown.

5 Serve stew and dumplings topped with extra parmesan; season with freshly ground pepper.

SWAP INS *Instead of pancetta, you could use bacon. Swap parmesan with another hard cheese, such as cheddar or Gruyère.*

ADD AN EGG

HIGHLY VERSATILE AND ENORMOUSLY YUMMY, EGGS CAN CONVERT LEFTOVERS AND PANTRY STAPLES INTO A MEAL IN MINUTES. ADJUST AND SWAP INGREDIENTS ACCORDING TO WHAT YOU HAVE AVAILABLE.

PESTO SCRAMBLED EGGS

PREP + COOK TIME 10 MINUTES **SERVES** 2

Halve 100g cherry tomatoes. Whisk 4 eggs and ⅓ cup (80ml) milk in a medium jug. Heat 1 tablespoon olive oil in a large frying pan over low heat. Cook egg mixture for 20 seconds or until gently set around the edge. Stir for 30 seconds or until eggs are just cooked. Remove from heat; season to taste. Serve on thick toast, topped with pesto (see page 96), halved cherry tomatoes and crumbled soft cheese; season to taste.

VEGETABLE EGG CURRY

PREP + COOK TIME 20 MINUTES **SERVES** 4

Cook 8 eggs in a saucepan of boiling water for 7 minutes. Transfer to a bowl of iced water; cool then peel. Meanwhile, heat 1½ tablespoons neutral oil and 3 tablespoons curry paste (see page 99) in a frying pan over medium-high heat; cook for 1 minute or until fragrant. Add 3 cups (450g) chopped mixed vegetables, 400ml can coconut milk, 2 teaspoons sugar and 1 tablespoon fish sauce; cook for 8 minutes or until vegies are just tender. Add eggs; cook for 1 minute or until warmed through. Stir in 1 tablespoon lime juice and season. Serve with roti and lime wedges.

OKONOMIYAKI

PREP + COOK TIME 20 MINUTES **SERVES** 2

Combine 2 cups (300g) coarsely grated firm vegetables, 2 sliced green onions, 1 clove crushed garlic, 4 eggs, 2 teaspoons soy sauce, 1 teaspoon sesame oil and 2 tablespoons plain flour in a large bowl; season. Heat 2 tablespoons neutral oil in a large frying pan over medium-heat; spread mixture evenly over the base of the pan. Cook for 3 minutes each side or until cooked through. To serve, drizzle with Japanese mayonnaise and tonkatsu sauce; sprinkle with bonito flakes, fried shallots, furikake and sliced green onion.

BAKED EGGS & BEANS

PREP + COOK TIME 15 MINUTES **SERVES** 2

Combine 2 cups (400g) canned beans, 400ml jar passata, 1 teaspoon sugar, 1 teaspoon smoked paprika and 1 teaspoon cumin seeds in a frying pan; cook over medium-high heat, stirring occasionally, for 5 minutes or until heated through. Season to taste. Using a spoon, make four indents in the sauce; crack 1 egg into each indent. Cover with a lid or foil. Cook for 5 minutes or until egg whites are set and yolks are cooked to your liking. Top with parsley and serve with grilled sourdough.

PREP + COOK TIME 1 HOUR 15 MINUTES **SERVES** 6

AVOCADO & CHOCOLATE SELF-SAUCING PUDDING

USE UP ANY OVER-RIPE OR FORGOTTEN AVOCADOS BY DISGUISING THEM IN THIS RICH CHOCOLATE SAUCE-LADENED DESSERT. THIS PUDDING IS MADE WITH 2 MEDIUM AVOCADOS (500G).

100g butter, softened, plus extra to grease
¼ cup (60ml) milk (see swap ins)
1 tbsp instant coffee
2 cups (320g) leftover chopped avocado (see note above)
1 egg
2 tsp vanilla paste (see swap ins)
½ tsp fine salt
1 cup (220g) firmly packed brown sugar
1¼ cups (175g) self-raising flour
¼ cup (25g) cocoa powder, plus extra for dusting
whipped cream or ice-cream and mixed berries (see swap ins), to serve

SAUCE

⅓ cup (35g) cocoa powder
½ cup (110g) firmly packed brown sugar
1 tbsp instant coffee

1 Preheat oven to 180°C/160°C fan-forced. Grease a 1.5-litre (6-cup) oval baking dish with extra butter.

2 Combine milk and coffee in a small bowl. Set aside for 5 minutes.

3 Blend or process avocado, butter, egg, vanilla, salt and sugar until smooth. Add coffee mixture, flour and cocoa; process until well combined.

4 Place the baking dish on an oven tray; pour in the chocolate batter.

5 Make the sauce: Combine cocoa and sugar in a small bowl; evenly scatter mixture over the chocolate batter. Combine coffee and 1¾ cups (430ml) boiling water in a jug. Pour coffee over the back of a large spoon all over the chocolate batter.

6 Bake pudding for 50 minutes or until it is firm and springs back when pressed.

7 Serve pudding topped with whipped cream or ice-cream and berries; dust with extra cocoa.

SWAP INS *We used full-cream milk, but use whatever milk is your preference. Instead of vanilla paste, you could use vanilla extract. Serve with whatever fruit is in season, such as sliced stone fruit or citrus segments.*

SAUCY

CREAMY

PREP + COOK TIME 25 MINUTES **SERVES** 4

CREAMY AVOCADO PASTA

INSTEAD OF CURLY FETTUCCINE, YOU COULD USE WHICHEVER PASTA YOU HAVE ON HAND. THE PASTA SAUCE REQUIRES THE EQUIVALENT OF 3 AVOCADOS (750G).

500g dried curly fettuccine (see note above)
2¼ cups (480g) leftover avocado, mashed (see note above)
⅔ cup (160ml) olive oil
2 bunches basil, stems and leaves, plus extra leaves to serve
1½ cups (120g) finely grated parmesan
1 tbsp finely grated lemon rind
¼ cup (60ml) lemon juice
⅔ cup (100g) pine nuts, toasted (see swap ins)

1 Cook pasta following packet directions. Reserve 1 cup (250ml) pasta water, then drain. Return pasta to pan.

2 Meanwhile, blend or process avocado, oil, basil, parmesan, lemon rind and juice until smooth; season to taste.

3 Add avocado sauce and ½ cup (125ml) of the reserved pasta water to the pasta; stir until the pasta is well coated and sauce is glossy, adding more pasta water as needed. Season to taste.

4 Serve pasta and sauce topped with pine nuts and extra basil leaves; season with freshly ground pepper.

SWAPS INS *Instead of pine nuts, you could use whichever nuts or seeds you have on hand.*

PREP + COOK TIME 1 HOUR (+ STANDING & REFRIGERATION) **SERVES** 4

ANY-VEGIE TART

IF YOU HAVE ANY WOODY HERBS ON HAND, SUCH AS THYME, OREGANO OR SAGE, RUB THEM INTO THE PASTRY WITH THE FLOUR, OR STIR THROUGH THE SLOW-COOKED ONIONS.

2 tbsp olive oil
1 large red onion (250g), sliced thinly
400g leftover cooked vegies
60g goat's cheese, crumbled
salad leaves and balsamic dressing, to serve

PASTRY

2 tbsp white chia seeds
1½ cups (225g) plain flour
1 tsp salt flakes
50g cold butter, cubed
1 egg, beaten lightly
¼ cup (60ml) olive oil

1 Make the pastry: Combine chia seeds and 2 tablespoons warm water in a small bowl. Stand for 20 minutes. Process chia mixture, flour, salt, butter, egg and oil until the dough just comes together. Shape pastry into a disc. Cover and refrigerate for 30 minutes.

2 Meanwhile, heat the oil in a large frying pan over low heat. Cook onion, stirring occasionally, for 20 minutes or until softened and caramelised; season to taste. Set aside to cool.

3 Preheat oven to 200°C/180°C fan-forced.

4 Roll the pastry between two sheets of baking paper into a 30cm round; fold in the edge to create a 1cm border. Transfer on the paper to an oven tray.

5 Bake pastry for 12 minutes or until golden. Spread the caramelised onion over the pastry base; top with cooked vegies and goat's cheese. Return tart to the oven; bake for a further 10 minutes or until vegies are heated through.

6 Serve tart topped with salad leaves and drizzled with balsamic dressing; season with freshly ground pepper.

SWAP INS

INSTEAD OF BACON, YOU COULD USE OTHER CURED PORK, SUCH AS SALAMI OR PROSCIUTTO. INSTEAD OF CHEDDAR, YOU COULD USE WHICHEVER CHEESE YOU HAVE ON HAND, SUCH AS PARMESAN, FETTA OR BRIE.

PREP + COOK TIME 1 HOUR 15 MINUTES (+ STANDING) **MAKES** 8

CHEESE & BACON VEGIE BAPS

INSTEAD OF LEFTOVER VEGIES, YOU COULD USE BOTTLED ROASTED OR MARINATED VEGIES, SUCH AS CAPSICUM, SEMI-DRIED TOMATOES, OLIVES AND ARTICHOKES.

2 tsp (7g) dried yeast
1 tsp caster sugar
1 cup (250ml) milk
60g butter, chopped
3 cups (480g) bread flour, plus extra for dusting
1 tsp fine salt
1 egg, beaten lightly
1 tbsp olive oil
4 rindless bacon slices (260g) (see swap ins)
400g leftover cooked vegetables (see note above)
1 cup (120g) grated cheddar (see swap ins)
butter, to serve

1 Combine yeast, ¼ cup (60ml) warm water and the sugar in a small bowl. Stand in a warm place for 10 minutes or until frothy.

2 Meanwhile, place milk and butter in a small saucepan; heat over low heat until butter is just melted and milk is warm but not hot.

3 Place half the flour and the salt in a large bowl, then add warm milk mixture, yeast mixture and egg; mix until combined. Add remaining flour and mix until well combined.

4 Turn dough out onto a lightly floured surface; knead for 10 minutes or until smooth and elastic (see tip). Transfer to a large, oiled bowl. Cover and stand in a warm place for 1 hour or until doubled in size.

5 Preheat oven to 180°C/160°C fan-forced.

6 Heat oil in a medium frying pan over high heat. Cook bacon for 1 minute each side or until browned. Drain on paper towel. Tear into large pieces.

7 Punch down dough in bowl, then turn out onto a lightly floured surface; knead for 1 minute or until smooth. Flatten dough out; arrange cooked vegetables, bacon and cheddar over one half. Fold dough over to cover the filling; gently knead, being careful not to break the vegetables too much, until just combined.

8 Divide dough into eight equal portions; shape each into a round. Place rounds in a wreath shape on a lined oven tray; dust with a little extra flour. Cover and stand in a warm place for 10 minutes or until slightly risen.

9 Bake rolls for 40 minutes or until hollow sounding when tapped; cover with foil for the last 10 minutes of baking to prevent overbrowning.

10 Serve rolls warm with butter.

TIP *If you have a stand mixer with a dough hook, knead dough on medium speed for 8 minutes or until smooth and elastic; the dough will be sticky.*

GLOSSARY

ALMONDS flat, pointy-tipped nuts with a pitted brown shell enclosing a creamy white kernel which is covered by a brown skin.
meal ground almonds; almonds are powdered to a coarse flour-like texture.
ANCHOVIES small oily fish. Anchovy fillets are preserved and packed in oil or salt in small cans or jars and are strong in flavour. Fresh anchovies are much milder.
BAKING POWDER a raising agent consisting mainly of two parts cream of tartar to one part bicarbonate of soda.
BAY LEAVES aromatic leaves from the bay tree, available fresh or dried; adds a strong, slightly peppery flavour.
BEETROOT firm, round root vegetable.
BICARBONATE OF SODA a raising agent.
BURGHUL also called bulghur wheat; hulled steamed wheat kernels that, once dried, are crushed into various sized grains.
BUTTER use salted or unsalted butter; 125g is equal to one stick of butter.
BUTTERMILK originally the term given to the slightly sour liquid left after butter was churned, today it is made from no-fat or low-fat milk to which specific bacterial cultures have been added.
CARDAMOM a spice native to India; can be purchased in pod, seed or ground form. It has a distinctive aromatic, sweetly rich flavour.
CHEESE
blue mould-treated cheeses mottled with blue veining.
cheddar the most common cow's milk 'tasty' cheese; should be aged, hard and have a pronounced bite.
fetta Greek in origin; a crumbly textured goat- or sheep-milk cheese, with a sharp, salty taste. Ripened and stored in salted whey.
goat's made from goat's milk; it has an earthy, strong taste. Available in soft, crumbly and firm textures, in various shapes and sizes, and sometimes rolled in ash or herbs.
Gruyère a hard-rind Swiss cheese with small holes and a nutty, slightly salty flavour.
haloumi a firm, cream-coloured sheep-milk cheese matured in brine; haloumi can be grilled or fried, briefly, without breaking down. Should be eaten while still warm as it becomes tough and rubbery on cooling.
mascarpone an Italian fresh cultured-cream product made in much the same way as yoghurt. Whiteish to creamy yellow in colour, with a buttery-rich, luscious texture.
mozzarella soft, spun-curd Italian cheese; traditionally made from water-buffalo milk. Now generally made from cow's milk, it is the most popular pizza cheese because of its low melting point and elasticity when heated.
parmesan also called parmigiano; is a hard, grainy cow's milk cheese originating in Italy. Reggiano is the best variety.
ricotta a soft, sweet, moist, white cow's milk cheese with a low fat content and a slightly grainy texture. The name roughly translates as 'cooked again' and refers to ricotta's manufacture from a whey that is itself a by-product of other cheese-making.
CHIA SEEDS contain protein and all the essential amino acids and a wealth of vitamins, minerals and antioxidants, as well as being fibre rich.
CHICKPEAS an irregularly round, sandy-coloured legume. Has a firm texture even after cooking, a floury mouth-feel and robust nutty flavour. Available canned or dried (soak for several hours in cold water before use).
CHILLI
flakes also sold as crushed chilli; dehydrated deep-red extremely fine slices and whole seeds.
long red available both fresh and dried; a generic term used for any moderately hot, long chilli (about 6–8cm long).
powder the Asian variety is the hottest, made from dried ground Thai chillies; can be used instead of fresh in the proportion of ½ teaspoon chilli powder to 1 medium chopped fresh red chilli.

CHOCOLATE, DARK also called luxury chocolate; made of a high percentage of cocoa liquor and cocoa butter, and little added sugar.

CINNAMON available both in the piece (called sticks or quills) and ground into powder; one of the world's most common spices, used universally as a sweet, fragrant flavouring for both sweet and savoury foods.

COCOA POWDER also known as unsweetened cocoa; cocoa beans (cacao seeds) that have been fermented, roasted, shelled, ground into powder then cleared of most of the fat content.

COCONUT

cream obtained commercially from the first pressing of the coconut flesh alone, without the addition of water; the second pressing (less rich) is sold as coconut milk.

milk not the liquid inside (coconut water) but the diluted liquid from the second pressing of the white flesh of a mature coconut.

oil is extracted from the coconut flesh so you don't get any of the fibre, protein or carbohydrates present in the whole coconut.

shredded thin strips of dried coconut.

CORNFLOUR available made from corn or wheat (wheaten cornflour gives a lighter texture in cakes); used as a thickening agent in cooking.

CREAM

pouring also called pure or fresh cream. It has no additives and contains a minimum fat content of 35%.

sour a thick, commercially-cultured sour cream with a minimum fat content of 35%.

thickened a whipping cream that contains a thickener; it has a minimum fat content of 35%.

CUMIN also known as zeera or comino; resembling caraway in size, cumin is the dried seed of a plant related to the parsley family. Available dried as seeds or ground.

FENNEL also called finocchio or anise; a crunchy green vegetable slightly resembling celery that's eaten raw in salads or cooked as an ingredient.

FISH SAUCE also called nam pla or nuoc nam; made from pulverised salted fermented fish, most often anchovies. Has a pungent smell and strong taste, so use sparingly.

FLOUR

plain all-purpose unbleached wheat flour; is the best for baking, as the gluten content ensures a strong dough for a light result.

self-raising all-purpose flour with baking powder and salt added; make at home in the proportion of 1 cup flour to 2 teaspoons baking powder.

GARAM MASALA a blend of spices that includes cardamom, cinnamon, coriander, cloves, fennel and cumin. Black pepper and chilli can also be added for heat.

GHEE clarified butter; with the milk solids removed, this fat has a high smoking point so can be heated to a high temperature without burning. Used as a cooking medium in most Indian recipes.

HARISSA a North African paste made from dried red chillies, garlic, olive oil and caraway seeds; can be used as a rub for meat, an ingredient in sauces and dressings or eaten as a condiment.

HONEY the variety sold in a squeezable container is not suitable for the recipes in this book.

MAPLE SYRUP distilled from the sap of sugar maple trees found only in Canada and the USA. Maple-flavoured syrup or pancake syrup is not an adequate substitute for the real thing.

MISO fermented soybean paste. There are many types of miso, each with its own aroma, flavour, colour and texture. It can be kept, airtight, for up to a year in the fridge. Generally, the darker the miso the saltier the taste and denser the texture. Buy in tubs or plastic packs.

NIGELLA SEEDS also known as kalonji or black onion seeds. Tiny, angular seeds, black on the outside and creamy within, with a sharp nutty flavour. Typically sprinkled over Turkish bread immediately after baking or as an important spice in Indian cooking; often erroneously called black cumin seeds.

NORI a type of dried seaweed used in Japanese cooking as a flavouring, garnish or for sushi. Sold in thin sheets, plain or toasted (yaki-nori).

OIL

coconut *see* Coconut

olive made from ripened olives. Extra virgin and virgin are the first and second press, respectively, of the olives; 'light' refers to taste not fat levels.

sesame used as a flavouring rather than a cooking oil.
vegetable oils sourced from plant rather than animal fats.

ONION
brown and white are interchangeable; white onions have a more pungent flesh.
green also called, incorrectly, shallot; an immature onion picked before the bulb has formed, with a long, green stalk.
red also known as Spanish or Bermuda onion; a sweet-flavoured, large, purple-red onion.
shallots also called French or golden shallots or eschalots; small and brown-skinned.

PANCETTA an Italian unsmoked bacon, pork belly cured in salt and spices then rolled into a sausage shape and dried for several weeks.

PINE NUTS also called pignoli; not a nut but a small, cream-coloured kernel from pine cones. Best toasted before use to bring out the flavour.

SICHUAN PEPPERCORNS also called Szechuan or Chinese pepper, native to the Sichuan province of China. A mildly hot spice that comes from the prickly ash tree. Although not related to the peppercorn family, these small, red-brown aromatic Sichuan berries look like peppercorns and have a distinctive peppery-lemon flavour and aroma.

STAR ANISE dried star-shaped pod with an astringent aniseed flavour; used to flavour stocks and marinades. Available whole and ground, it is an essential ingredient in five-spice powder.

STERILISING JARS it's important the jars be as clean as possible; make sure your hands, the preparation area, tea towels and cloths etc. are clean too. The aim is to finish sterilising the jars and lids at the same time the mixture is ready to be bottled; the hot mixture should be bottled into hot, dry, clean jars. Jars that aren't sterilised properly can cause deterioration of the contents during storage. Always start with cleaned washed jars and lids, then follow one of these methods:
(1) Put the jars and lids through the hottest cycle of a dishwasher without using any detergent.
(2) Lie the jars down in a boiler with the lids, cover with cold water, then cover with a lid. Bring to the boil over high heat and boil the jars for 20 minutes.
(3) Stand the jars upright, without touching each other, on a wooden board on the lowest oven shelf. Turn the oven to the lowest possible temperature; leave jars to heat for 30 minutes.
Remove jars from the oven or dishwasher with a tea towel, or from the boiling water with tongs and rubber-gloved hands; the water will evaporate from hot wet jars quite quickly. Stand jars upright, and not touching each other, on a wooden board or a bench covered with a tea towel. Fill jars as directed in the recipe; secure the lids tightly, holding jars firmly with a tea towel or an oven mitt. Leave the jars at room temperature to cool before storing.

SUGAR
brown very soft, finely granulated sugar retaining molasses for its characteristic colour and flavour.
caster finely granulated table sugar.
demerara small-grained golden crystal sugar.

SUMAC a purple-red, astringent spice ground from berries growing on shrubs flourishing wild around the Mediterranean; adds a tart, lemony flavour to food.

TAHINI a rich, sesame seed paste, used in most Middle Eastern cuisines, especially Lebanese, in dips and sauces.

TURMERIC also called kamin; is a rhizome related to galangal and ginger. Must be grated or pounded to release its acrid aroma and pungent flavour. Known for the golden colour it imparts, fresh turmeric can be substituted with the more commonly found dried powder. When fresh turmeric is called for in a recipe, the dried powder can be substituted (1 teaspoon of ground turmeric for every 20g of fresh turmeric).

VANILLA BEAN PASTE made from vanilla beans and containing real seeds; is highly concentrated: 1 teaspoon replaces a whole vanilla bean.

VINEGAR
cider made from fermented apples.
rice wine made from rice wine lees (sediment left after fermentation), salt and alcohol.
wine based on red or white wine.

YEAST (dried and fresh) a raising agent used in dough-making. Granular (7g sachets) and fresh compressed (20g blocks) yeast can almost always be substituted one for the other.

CONVERSION CHART

MEASURES

One Australian metric measuring cup holds approximately 250ml; one Australian metric tablespoon holds 20ml; one Australian metric teaspoon holds 5ml.

The difference between one country's measuring cups and another's is within a two- or three-teaspoon variance and will not affect your cooking results. North America, New Zealand and the United Kingdom use a 15ml tablespoon.

All cup and spoon measurements are level. The most accurate way of measuring dry ingredients is to weigh them. When measuring liquids, use a clear glass or plastic jug with the metric markings.

Measurements for cake pans are approximate only. Using same-shaped cake pans of a similar size should not affect the outcome of your baking. We measure the inside top of the cake pan to determine size.

We use extra-large eggs with an average weight of 60g.

DRY MEASURES

METRIC	IMPERIAL
15g	½oz
30g	1oz
60g	2oz
90g	3oz
125g	4oz (¼lb)
155g	5oz
185g	6oz
220g	7oz
250g	8oz (½lb)
280g	9oz
315g	10oz
345g	11oz
375g	12oz (¾lb)
410g	13oz
440g	14oz
470g	15oz
500g	16oz (1lb)
750g	24oz (1½lb)
1kg	32oz (2lb)

LIQUID MEASURES

METRIC	IMPERIAL
30ml	1 fluid oz
60ml	2 fluid oz
100ml	3 fluid oz
125ml	4 fluid oz
150ml	5 fluid oz
190ml	6 fluid oz
250ml	8 fluid oz
300ml	10 fluid oz
500ml	16 fluid oz
600ml	20 fluid oz
1000ml (1 litre)	1¾ pints

LENGTH MEASURES

METRIC	IMPERIAL
3mm	⅛in
6mm	¼in
1cm	½in
2cm	¾in
2.5cm	1in
5cm	2in
6cm	2½in
8cm	3in
10cm	4in
13cm	5in
15cm	6in
18cm	7in
20cm	8in
22cm	9in
25cm	10in
28cm	11in
30cm	12in (1ft)

OVEN TEMPERATURES

The oven temperatures in this book are for conventional ovens;
if you have a fan-forced oven, decrease the temperature by 10–20 degrees.

	°C (CELSIUS)	°F (FAHRENHEIT)
VERY SLOW	120	250
SLOW	150	300
MODERATELY SLOW	160	325
MODERATE	180	350
MODERATELY HOT	200	400
HOT	220	425
VERY HOT	240	475

INDEX

PUBLISHED IN 2023 BY ARE MEDIA BOOKS, AUSTRALIA.
ARE MEDIA BOOKS IS A DIVISION OF ARE MEDIA PTY LIMITED.

ARE MEDIA

Chief Executive Officer Jane Huxley

ARE MEDIA BOOKS

Group Publisher Nicole Byers
Editorial & Food Director Sophia Young
Books Director David Scotto
Creative Director Hannah Blackmore
Managing Editor Stephanie Kistner
Art Director & Designer Kelsie Walker
Food Editor Bec Dickinson
Senior Editor Chantal Gibbs
Production Controller Kara Stead

Photographer James Moffatt
Stylist Lucy Busuttil
Photochefs Rebecca Lyall, Clare Maguire

Introduction & additional text
Gina Lopez, Environmental Consultant

Special thanks to Bed Threads and Fazeek for loaning Are Media props to use in the photoshoot. bedthreads.com.au, fazeek.com.au

womensweeklyfood
@womensweeklyfood

Printed in China by
Leo Paper Products

A catalogue record for this book is available from the National Library of Australia.
ISBN 978-1-76122-077-7 (paperback)

ABN 18 053 273 546

Published by Are Media Books,
a division of Are Media Pty Limited,
54 Park St, Sydney; GPO Box 4088,
Sydney, NSW 2001, Australia
Ph +61 2 9282 8000
www.awwcookbooks.com.au

International rights enquiries
internationalrights@aremedia.com.au

Order Books
Phone 1300 322 007 (within Australia)

Or order online at
www.awwcookbooks.com.au

Send recipe enquiries to
recipeenquiries@aremedia.com.au